Dave Langan:

Running Through Walls

Dave Langan:
Running Through Walls

With Trevor Keane & Alan Conway

DB PUBLISHING

First published in Great Britain in 2011 by The Derby Books Publishing Company Limited, 3 The Parker Centre, Derby, DE21 4SZ.

ISBN 978-1-7809-101-09

Printed and bound by Gomer

Contents

Acknowledgements

I would like to dedicate this book to my mother Clare, my late father Bill and my wife Dawn for all their support over the years. I would also like to dedicate this book to my three children, Elliot, Callum and Leah, I've not been the best of fathers but I do love you.

There are a number of people who have helped me, not just in getting this book together, but also at difficult times in my life and I would love to thank them for their help and support over the years: Audrey and Peter Lawless, Clare, Stephen and baby David Lawson, Siobhan Langan, Billy Langan, Jacinta Langan, Danny Larkin, Victoria and Takara Gordon and Margaret Powers, John Wilkes, Gerry Flynn and everyone at Cherry Orchard, Laro Byrne, the late Brian Clough, Maurice Evans, Jim Smith, Eoin Hand. John Giles, my old friend Pat Murtagh, Joe Corcoran, Cathal Dervan, Vincent Hogan, Conleth Meehan and his parents, Bernie and Michael Meehan, Phelim Warren and the lads from the Boys in Green who have been so good to me over the years and really championed my cause.

I also want to thank all my old club and International teammates for so many great memories and especially Ray Houghton, Niall Quinn, Paul McGrath, Trevor Hebberd, Don O'Riordan and Mick Harford who all provided some lovely interviews for this book.

I would also love to thank Mick Moore and his wife Sandra for their help and support over the years, not to mention for organising the benefit game for me in July 2011. I also want to thank Aileen Lawless, Stephen Byrne, Steve Brunnock, Tony Matthews and Craig Rogers. To all those I have missed out, I am very sorry.

Finally I would like to thank everyone at DB Publishing for giving me the opportunity to tell my story and to Trevor Keane and Alan Conway for taking my words and making them into a book.

I hope you enjoy the read.
Dave Langan

Foreword

By Vincent Hogan

One reason I wanted to write this foreword was to vent a little anger.

In 2008, when I penned a couple of articles about Dave Langan, the great vulgar circus that professional football had become seemed the obvious counterpoint to the story of a man, quite literally, broken up by the game.

All the bling and essential fakery of surly nonentities dragging home suitcases of money for, to put it kindly, unremarkable effort could not but antagonize when set against the awful personal circumstance of a man who once played the game (every game) as if defending his family's honour.

Yet, our revulsion at what football has become is getting a little hackneyed, isn't it?

Television money has corrupted the very concept of ambition, so can we honestly blame the kid who gets paid more in a week than the annual income of a teacher or policeman, if he does not come across as a particularly grounded member of society?

Anyway, Dave is probably tired of people trying to reconcile how a man capped 26 times for his country could end up sleeping in a Town Hall cupboard when a journeyman footballer today can, reputedly, park his Porsche at a Spanish train station and instantly forget he ever owned it.

It is pointless trying to make sense of it. Worse, it is patently unhealthy.

So I have chosen to decommission the anger. A curmudgeon's sermon from the mount would probably be to lose the point of Dave's story, to miss the essential humility and grace of a great football man who – at the height of the physical traumas that would have him registered as 'a cripple' – was asked one simple question.

'With the way you've ended up,' his surgeon once enquired, 'if you had your time back, would you do it all again?'

And Dave Langan replied, 'Without a shadow of a doubt, doc!'

One of my favourite Langan stories is that of him accompanying his somewhat reticent Oxford United club mates, John Aldridge and Ray Houghton, to Dublin for their international debuts with the Republic of Ireland. Neither had even been to the city before and seemed to struggle with the geography.

Both expressed fear that their accents might draw unfriendly attention given 'The Troubles', as we called them, seemed to be spawning almost weekly atrocities at the time.

Dave recalled having to reassure his Oxford teammates that Dublin and Belfast, albeit two cities existing fewer than a hundred miles apart, might as well have belonged in different galaxies.

That was 1986 and of course, within two years, the story of Jack Charlton's Ireland would take our national team to previously uncharted heights at Euro '88, with both Aldridge and Houghton in the vanguard.

Dave, as we know, never got to Germany. Even those who worshipped at the altar of 'Big Jack' could not but acknowledge his limitations as a communicator. Charlton might not ever have backed down from a challenge when he was playing but, in management, there were plenty of days when he ducked things.

I am sure the cack-handed way Dave's international career came to an end is well documented between the covers of this book. Suffice to say it was a travesty. Langan's body was already breaking down because of the selflessness shown on Irish duty in an extraordinary World Cup qualifier against France at Lansdowne Road seven years previously.

Yet, he was not granted even the simple courtesy of a phone call.

I remember that game as if it was last summer. This was an exotic French squad, one speckled with special footballers like Janvion, Larios, Platini and Six. But, on that October evening in '81, Langan terrorized anyone in a blue shirt who had a mind to explore the right side of Ireland's defence.

Dave was not big or broad, you see. But, with socks down around his ankles, he played with the ferocity of a hungry guard-dog.

We now know that his calamitous injury woes can be traced back to that evening, yet Dave just took himself home to his Ma's house in Ringsend afterwards, all pain dulled by the adrenaline of a famous 3–2 victory.

He had damaged knee cartilage, though, and – as the problem subsequently became chronic – the physical stress of his rehab programme would lead to him cracking a vertebra in his back.

We can but imagine the subsequent loneliness, the stark sense of being forgotten, that flooded through his days then as career and home life splintered into a thousand unhappy pieces.

Dave's story needed to be told because, if nothing else, it will stand on bookshelves as a defiant, compelling voice against the bland narrative of Mills and Boon biographies that seem obligatory now for any footballer old enough to drive.

I was surprised and privileged to be asked to write this foreword. Maybe a lifetime in sports journalism pickles the mind in cynicism. You become fatigued from all the bullshit and preciousness that pass for professional dialogue between those who strive for the big prizes and those employed to chronicle the struggle.

Dave Langan's story is an antidote to that fatigue.

Football did not make him rich and, in the end, it probably broke his heart. But there was a time when he played the game as furiously as any man on the planet. Those of us who saw it were the lucky ones.

Vincent Hogan (*Irish Independent*), November 2011.

Dave Langan

A fan's appreciation

Legend, star, hero; three often and much over-used nouns to describe footballers particularly in the media-saturated coverage of football today. They are, however, three nouns that only go some way to describing my opinion and memory of Dave Langan the footballer.

Dave made his Irish debut against Turkey in 1978 in a 4–2 victory at Lansdowne Road and it was one of my earliest matches as an Ireland fan (I was 11 at the time).

My footballing memories however, remain pretty vivid as a still passionate 45-year-old Ireland fan and my memories of Dave Langan will always remain ingrained in my mind, more than most players who have worn our beloved green shirt.

You see Dave was one of our own. He hails from Ringsend, a mere Dave Langan clearance away from Lansdowne Road and he played in that quintessentially Irish way, displaying a fearless heart that endeared him to not only Irish fans, but to the fans of the clubs he played for in England.

Dave would tackle as if his life and his nation's fate depended on it; he charged up and down the right flank in that inimitable and unmistakeable gallop that was uniquely Dave. He sweated blood and too many tears for us but let's not forget that as well as his fearsome commitment, Dave Langan was a bloody good footballer. Brian Clough would not have given him a second look if he was not.

He would not evoke fond memories from fans of Derby County, Birmingham City and Oxford United if he could not play. Oh yes, Dave Langan could certainly play and the centre-forwards such as Frank Stapleton and John Aldridge to whom he provided numerous assists for goals would also testify to that.

One goal I remember in particular was a World Cup Qualifier at Lansdowne against Switzerland in 1985. An early free-kick from Kevin Sheedy spotted Dave haring down the right flank on the West Stand side.

Sheedy's floated cross-field pass was met on the volley by Dave and the ball fizzed across the Swiss goalmouth for Stapleton to score a crucial early opener. Ireland won 3–0 that day.

One Diego Armando Maradona could also vouch for Dave's existence in the early stages of Maradona's remarkable career as Dave got close enough to be able to kick the Argentinean genius at Lansdowne Road. It was a charity match in name only!

The above is only the tip of the iceberg as to why I loved Dave Langan as a player.

Sadly, despite playing in many of the Euro '88 qualifiers under Jack Charlton, Dave was deemed surplus to requirements by Charlton who brought in John Anderson as cover instead. The rest as they say is history as Euro '88 marked the birth of relative success for the Irish football team and Dave Langan quickly faded into oblivion as we all got carried away on Charlton's runaway train across Germany, Italy and USA in terms of successful qualifications for European Championships and World Cups.

Not only did Dave miss out on those wonderful experiences at Finals, he missed out on a Testimonial from the FAI. Previously, 25 caps was enough to be granted a Testimonial but the FAI increased it to 50 as the breakup of the Soviet Union and other nations led to an increasing number of international matches.

Dave won 26 caps for his country but the conditions were changed when Dave had attained 25. It was tough on Dave, but the footballing Gods in the latter part of Dave's career had been very tough indeed.

His knee injury in that memorable 3–2 win over France in 1981 at Lansdowne was the catalyst to the chronic injury problems that are catalogued in this book and missing out on Euro '88 was the final kick in the guts for Dave on top of his knee and back trouble. Dave was forgotten, but thankfully, if belatedly, he would again be remembered.

A chance conversation between Conleth Meehan and his father Michael about Irish players led to Dave Langan's name being mentioned by Michael. Michael told his son how Dave Langan lit up Lansdowne Road with his savage commitment and 100 per cent honesty and Michael mentioned how it was terribly unfair that Dave had missed out on footballing glory and no little finance having served his country with distinction and having been injured on Ireland duty.

The feeling of injustice grew inside Conleth Meehan who logged onto Irish Fans' website You Boys in Green and highlighted Dave's plight and misfortune. Vincent Hogan from the Irish Independent noticed the topic on that website and penned an article, likening Dave's commitment to the Irish cause and his painful fall into financial and physical ruin with the selfish, arrogant and childish demeanour of Stephen Ireland, who at that time was holding media court over his disgraceful attitude to playing for his country. Hogan's article hit home.

Irish fans who saw Dave remembered what he meant to them. Fans that did not see him play were angered by his plight when compared with the selfish, mollycoddled and disgusting behaviour of too many of today's so-called stars. Fans decided Dave Langan would be properly remembered and suitably honoured.

Conleth visited Dave's family in Ringsend to find out more about him and through You Boys in Green, a campaign for the FAI to reward Dave with a Testimonial was started. The campaign very quickly grew legs. RTE's Liveline programme carried the story with interviews with Conleth and myself who spoke on Dave's behalf to highlight the injustice he had suffered. Dave himself spoke on the programme with huge emotion and typical self-effacement. Dave did not do bitterness, in public anyhow, he does not do offending anyone but his words on the Liveline show were heart-rending and bursting with honesty and humility. The fans' determination snowballed.

Meetings with the FAI were well received in fairness to Gerry McDermott and Mick Lawlor who listened to Conleth's plea for Dave to get his break. Progress was made and various other people lobbied for Dave to be recognised officially.

At half-time in Giovanni Trapattoni's first match as Irish manager against Serbia in May 2008, the Eircom Legend Award was presented to Dave Langan. This was only the start. After the match as fans assembled in Jury's Inn, You Boys in Green fans all wore 'Testimonial for Langan' T-shirts as awareness grew to a wider audience and fans mingled with the Eircom Legend recipient who remained unassuming and humble as ever.

Dave's richly deserved Testimonial Dinner was finally approved by the FAI and held in the Burlington Hotel on 11 October 2008.

Former teammates of Dave from the Irish team turned up to celebrate his long-overdue recognition, the likes of Liam Brady, Ray Houghton, Packie Bonner, Ray Houghton and Niall Quinn. Jimmy Magee was the consummate MC as numerous people spoke glowing words of tribute to Dave but it was the Guest of Honour whose words meant the most to the great gathering at the Burlington. Dave's gratitude was palpable, heartfelt and as always 100 per cent humble.

This night for him may have been 20 years late, but thanks to Conleth Meehan's conversation with his father, the testimonial finally happened and life was about to become financially a bit more stable for Dave and his lovely wife Dawn as a result.

Thankfully, contact has remained between the Meehans and the Langans and that friendship and the Testimonial enabled me to meet Dave and Dawn on several occasions. It is often said that one should not meet your heroes in case they disappoint. Well it's 100 per cent not true about Dave Langan.

Dave was a hero of mine on the football pitch and is a hero of mine to this day and I am honoured to have been able to meet Dave and Dawn. I am honoured to have been asked to write a passage for this book and it was Irish fans' honour to see Dave Langan play 26 times for Ireland.

Go n-éirí an t-ádh leat i gcónaí a Dhaithí!

Phelim Warren, Tallaght, Dublin.

October 2011.

Chapter One

Life as I know it

I have just finished watching the second leg of the Euro 2012 Play-off match, Ireland have just drawn with Estonia 1–1; the 4–0 away win in Tallinn setting the scene for one of the most relaxed evenings in competitive Irish football. The Irish team are on their way to the European Championship in Poland and the Ukraine in June 2012. The team had played brilliantly in the first leg to all but clinch their place and it has been a while since I have seen a more accomplished display away from home, especially in such an important match.

As an Irish fan I am delighted, these players deserve it, the likes of Shay Given, Richard Dunne and Robbie Keane are household names and deserve the chance to play on Europe's biggest stage. It is almost 24 years since an Irish team has qualified for the European Championships, back in 1988. I think back to that time and suddenly the joy I feel evaporates and I am drawn right back to a darker time. A time in my life when I was on the cusp of something brilliant only to have it snatched away from me.

I played in four of the qualifying games for Ireland on their way to the big adventure Euro '88 and I should have been on the plane to Germany, however, just like that I was excluded from the squad and missed out. Someone in this current group will miss out, be it through injury, loss of form or fall out. They will regret it for the rest of their lives.

Of course while not forgotten, those footballing days are in the past now, life is very different now to when I was a footballer, I remember in my first year as an apprentice, it was get up and race down to the Baseball Ground for 9am where we would get the kits ready and make tea for all the players and staff. The first team would train till lunchtime while we cleaned and got everything organised, and then they trained us in the afternoon before cleaning up again. The day ended at 5pm and then you would head back to the digs.

Nowadays it's up at 7am, my creaky knees barely making it out of bed.

My knees are very stiff and sometimes I worry that they will give way on my way down the stairs. Oddly enough it's my right knee that gives me more trouble than my left knee. I had eight operations on my left knee and none on my right, however there is more fluid in my right knee. It feels sometimes that my knees cannot support me and could collapse at any moment, getting out of the car causes the same sensation.

I take Arthrotec for the pain, it is for arthritic joints and it helps, I also have a form of arthritis in my hands and especially my thumb joint, which I have been told needs replacing. The hand and thumb are not related to the football however, they are just life. The knees and back are a constant reminder of football but, unlike medals, these are not memories I like to recall.

These days I work for the local council, in the Mayor's office. My job is very basic and thankfully not very challenging. I am required to make tea and coffee for the Mayor and any guests, I help the mayor put on his gown and I am often required to give a tour of the townhouse. I had to learn the history of the townhouse for this; I am still learning it to be honest.

I head into the Mayor's office for 7.30am and will sometimes work till midnight depending on how many guests he has on the day, although it can often be earlier. When I am finished work, myself and Dawn, my wife, go for a walk around a park that is right beside where I live. It is important to get a small bit of exercise for the knee and it keeps me relatively fit. There will come a day when I will not be able to do this walk. I worry at the thought of it.

Every three months I visit the surgeon for a check up, he keeps telling me that I need to walk more as it helps with the flexibility, I often think he forgets how much pain I am in. Sitting is not good for the knees I know that, they get stiff and I worry sometimes I will not be able to get up after sitting down. The surgeon has told me I need new knees but that means three to six months off work and I can not afford to do that at the moment.

I remember when I was over in Ireland for my FAI benefit dinner in October 2008 and afterwards Kevin Moran took me to see his brother Ray who is an orthopaedic surgeon. Ray had a look at my knees and did a MRI scan, basically he said that I needed to get new knees, but that I should try to hold off as long as I can as I would need new ones again in 10 years and again 10 years after that. He also had a look at my back, which is not as bad as my knees; he told me that I have a small hole in my back and when that closes up I am in big trouble.

The thought of that hole closing worries me an awful lot. I worry a lot these days, as does my wife; she worries that we need to move to a one-storey house, as soon enough I will not make it up the stairs and that the knees will give. Luckily the job is not very physical, it is not work really, it is very easy and very different from being a footballer but I am very grateful to have it and enjoy it.

If I was a footballer today I would have been made for life on the back of one good year. In my day it was different, you earned £250 a week, when Oxford won the Milk Cup we got £800 as a bonus; different money. You got paid £50 for playing for Ireland along with the airfare and any taxi costs, although let it be said I would have played for Ireland for nothing.

There were no football agents in those days and I think if I had representatives working for me then I might not have made some of the decisions I did. I remember when I signed for Birmingham, Jim Smith said to me, 'I'll give you the same as what you are on at Derby as well as £50 appearance money every game'.

I said, 'grand let's go'. It was all done in three minutes and then we went and had a lager. There was no guidance, no agents, it was a different world.

People think that because you were a footballer you're minted, sadly for a lot of footballers who missed out on the Premier League that is not the case. I played during the 1980s, which was a dark time in England, the country was in a recession and there was not a lot of money around the place. Even now I find it funny that England finds itself in a similar state yet still premiership footballers are getting big wage increases, I do not know any other industry where that would happen. There is certainly no tightening of the belts, although it is different outside of the Premier League, you see clubs going into administration almost every week; that was the realities we all faced back then. You never knew if you were safe or not.

It's funny but when you look at the bench nowadays, there are more people there than on the pitch, between substitutes, managers, coaches and, I hear they even have orthopaedic surgeons on some of them; so much has changed. A different era; we had steak and chips before a game, now it is all fruit and pasta.

I still watch the Match of the Day and follow the football, but it is different, Wayne Rooney aside there is no one that excites me, he is not much of role model but we all go off the rails at times; when he is on fire though no one can stop him. I remember Frank Worthington and Charlie George, the modern footballer would not lace the boots of these lads; they were showmen and they played to the crowd. Nowadays the footballers are not as in touch with the fans, unlike the likes of Frank and Charlie who would have a pint with fans, although I am not sure that was a wise thing to do.

When I finished as a footballer, there was no big insurance pay out; I had nothing. I was forced to go on the dole for a while, as I could not work because of my back. The doctor gave me a green card, which in the UK means you are registered disabled. I got a job with the council on the back of that and have been there for 20 years. I worked initially as a car park attendant, then in security, then as a porter before I finally settled in the Mayor's office.

My first job outside of football was working as a car park attendant, the job was terrible though and I hated it, I used to get slagged off something terrible by Peterborough fans. I had finished my career there and to be honest the Posh fans did not like me and never took to me. I never did any good for them you see, although my defence was that with the injuries I had I just was not able.

They would be shouting at me 'Look how far you've fallen'. I must admit I did feel embarrassed by it all but I needed the job, I had bills to pay and it was better than the dole.

Even now I still get Peterborough fans around here telling me I was crap. I try not to react and generally rise above it all, although one time I was out for a few drinks and was walking home when these two lads starting mouthing off at me, being brave with the drink I talked back and I ended up in a scrap with them that resulted in me going to casualty needing stitches. It was stupid, normally I would have kept my mouth shut but the few drinks made me talk back, I have learned to get used to it though and can ignore it now.

Given that the football fans of the area do not like me, it is strange that I still live in Peterborough. The simple reason I stayed here though is that when I signed for the club I was married with two kids and I bought a house here, my kids still live in the area and although I am estranged from the kids, I still want to be near them.

In footballing terms it is a strange story how I actually came to sign for them. John Devaney, who was a director at Oxford United when I was there, had become the chairman at Peterborough and he remembered me and said to Mick Jones (Peterborough manager) 'let's get Langy', as I was called back then.

I was at Bournemouth at the time with Harry Redknapp, and they allowed me to talk to Peterborough, so I travelled up. I spent six hours chatting with the club and in the end I was so hungry, you know the hunger when you cannot even think straight. I said to John, 'I'm starving' and he said, 'sure, sign this and we can have something to eat'. So I did.

I was injured a lot in those days and in the end the club paid out the final two years of my contract and gave me £9,000, which I put against the mortgage. There was a recession on then, much like now, so it was hard to sell the house and move on. I was stuck here.

I can see why the fans of Peterborough never took to me though; they never saw the best of me really. I remember one game in particular; sadly it was my last game in the English League. It was a midweek one and Mick Jones, the then manager, said he needed to include me in the squad. At the time I had a hamstring problem and told him I was not fit. Mick said, 'don't worry, it's only to put names on the bench, I won't need you'. Anyway sure enough, we are 1–0 down and the fans are going ballistic, so he asked me to go on, I told him again I was not fit, but he said just go out on the right wing and stay there and cross in a few balls. On I went and eight minutes later I had to come off; the abuse I got was horrendous. They saw it as me not trying, I was on the bench so I must have been fit, but I was not.

Afterwards Mick tried to fine me two weeks' wages for the coming off but I rang the PFA and they got involved and said it was not right and that I was unable to play. I try to avoid the chat with fans around here if I can, although you will get someone that will often ask who was the most difficult opponent you have marked and when I reply 'Maradona' then the conversation goes a different way and it is great.

I will still get letters from fans of Oxford, Birmingham and Derby mind, I recently got one from a Derby fan living in Peterborough who wrote to the council, who passed it on. He wanted to know if I would sign some books and tops for him. I said no problem and we met up. I had a great rapport with those fans, they took me to their hearts and they appreciated that I gave 120 per cent each time I got on the pitch. They knew that I went into tackles I probably should not have gone for, headed balls that I probably should not have headed and they knew that every time I came off the pitch I was physically exhausted because I would run and run and run.

As my dad used to say to me, 'no matter what, always give 120 per cent and they will forgive you, no matter how bad the result'.

Just as the book was being finalised and getting ready to go the publisher, I got the news that I had been waiting to hear for a while. The orthopaedic surgeon has asked me to sign the consent form to allow him to make a new knee for me; I have been through a lot of operations these last 30 years but I am probably more scared now than on all those other occasions put together. The doctor is a nice guy; he even said he would buy a copy of this book when it comes out. He told me that it needs to be done, I trust him; even though he is a Manchester City supporter. I know myself it needs doing anyway, but that doesn't make it any easier though, He has also said that he will do my other knee when the time is right, basically I will be 55 and both my knees will have been replaced.

It's a big operation, I will be out of action for three months, and will not be able to work but once it's healed I will be in considerably less pain than I am in nowadays, which will be good.

In all I have had 11 operations, eight on my left knee and three on my back, the first operation I had was on my knee and the two new knees will take the operation count to 13, unlucky for some but hopefully that will not be the case for me. I missed 18 months from February 1983 to the summer of 1984 when I was released by Birmingham. During my career I was so eager to play I took a lot of cortisone injections, which definitely did not help because I should have let nature take its course rather than rushing back into action too soon. My own eagerness was often my undoing, the cracked vertebra, sustained in the gym, needlessly throwing myself in to every tackle, pushing myself to get back onto the pitch and play and staying on the pitch when I should have come off.

Chapter Two

From Ringsend to Derby

My first memory of football was with my father down in Ringsend Park when I was five, we used to play with an old leather ball; you know, the ones with laces, and we would have a kick around every Sunday after Mass. Word soon spread locally of the kick around and soon there was a 15-a-side game being played every Sunday, then the game moved to before Mass when we would play from 9am to 12pm.

We used have coats for goals; it was great fun and it really got football into my blood. From then on that was all I wanted to play, I would kick a ball against the side wall of the house, often breaking windows in the process and when I had burst a ball, my Ma would go and get me another one.

I would play challenge matches as we called them against lads from the Ringsend Flats; they were always good competitive games. Sometimes the ball would go flying into the Dodder, a river that flows through the back of Ringsend along the side of Lansdowne Road, and I can tell you we took some chances getting the ball back, scary at times. The games were great though, they were competitive but there was never any fighting or anything, it was all in good spirits.

Afterwards we would sit and chat about the game. My best friends in those days were Peter Downey, Steven Scanlon, John Fox, Paddy Murtagh, Tony Gaffney and Gino Lawless. Gino was a great player and enjoyed great success with Bohemians and Dundalk; he won a couple of League Championships and Cups. He could have played at a higher level too, he was that good.

John and Steven sadly passed away from illnesses a few years ago. It was very sad to hear of their passing, as we were all very close growing up though.

Manchester United was the team that everyone supported in those days and with players like George Best, Bobby Charlton, Denis Law and Paddy Crerand it was easy to see why. You would hear the games on the radio in those days and get all the football magazines. All the lads would fight to be Best and Charlton when we were playing our little games, they were the players everyone wanted to be and we did not even know what they were like off the pitch.

Despite supporting Manchester United as a kid, Arsenal and Northern Ireland legend Pat Jennings was my hero growing up. When we used to play and practice up by the Dodder whenever anyone had to go in goal they were always Pat Jennings. I could not believe it years later when I got to play against him and even managed to score against him. Naturally I also loved watching Best and would try to emulate his skills. He was unbelievable and probably the sole reason why so many kids in Ireland supported United. I actually got to meet him once when I was at Birmingham, he was with Angie at the time and was off the drink, in fact he drank nothing but water that evening. I got to speak to him and it was definitely one of the highlights of my life, it's always nice to get to meet a hero and I was lucky enough to.

I would still hear from Paddy Murtagh, he often calls into my mother when he is down in Ringsend. I actually had my first gamble with Paddy, we put 10 pence on a horse and the worst thing that could have possibly have happened to me did, the horse won. If that horse had lost I might have learned a valuable lesson but sadly it came in and we had money to go to the pictures. I took the gambling with me to England.

Football was our thing and it bonded us up, for me though it was in my blood and I trained every day, I could not stop if I wanted to, I just wanted to kick a ball. I remember the school I went to at the time was very big into Gaelic Football and Hurling. In those days you had to play them too before you would be allowed to play soccer and even then playing the 'garrison game' was frowned upon.

I got involved with both the Gaelic Football and the Hurling teams for Star of the Sea, I enjoyed both sports. I remember playing a semi-final Gaelic football match for Star of the Sea and I played a game against a team from down the country and I had an experience that put me off the game for life. One of the opposition knocked me clean out, the physicality of it put me off, it is a tough sport. I loved hurling though and was good at it too, I used to play up front and scored lots of goals, but for me soccer was my first love.

I remember one time I got in serious trouble because of my love of playing soccer, Mr Cooling was a teacher at our school and him and a parish priest saw me playing a two-on-two game with Paul Flood, Fran Flood and Richie Boland. We were called in front of everyone at assembly and given what we called 'six of the best', which were three lashes of the cane in one hand and then another three on the other hand. Mr Cooling said me to me, 'you had better learn your lesson Langan, you have no chance of being a footballer and you're wasting your time. You need to learn your lessons to get a good job', but I was so infatuated with football I never listened. Looking back now he was right, I wished I had studied and gotten a qualification.

If my Dad was my first influence on my career then it safe to say that Lar O'Byrne was the second. Lar had played for Shamrock Rovers and Drumcondra FC as well Ireland in the 1940s and 1950s and was the coach of Bath Rangers, my local team and my first team. Lar was a big influence on my career and he started me in the centre of midfield, it would be Colin Murphy who would later move me to right-back where I made my name but Lar started me in midfield. I started playing with Bath Rangers for their Under-12 team, I was always a bit low on confidence but Lar would tell me I played great even if I was rubbish.

At that time my Ma would head down to the markets on Thomas Street where she would buy my boots, in those days we lived off about 30 bob a week and boots cost £1.50 so my Ma would bargain with the market trader to get the boots. They never lasted long though and no sooner had I got a pair than I needed another. Lar arranged for me to get a very good pair of new boots, which was great not just for me but also for my Ma. He was very good to me and always kept in touch with me over the years.

At Bath Rangers I had moved up the ages groups and was playing for the under-15 side as well as the Irish schoolboy side who at that time were managed by Mick Byrne and Billy Young. One particular trip would have a big influence on my career; we were travelling over to a game against Wales and were on the boat. John Wilkes, who was the manager of Cherry Orchard and also, I would later learn, a Derby County scout, came over to me and said, 'what are you doing next year?' to which I replied, 'playing for Bath Rangers' he then said 'come play with us'. I decided to stay where I was though. I remember though the night before the season began I was down having a kick around when John and Gerry Flynn, who was a co-manager with John, came down in their car to me. Gerry said to me, 'Are you all there son, are you really going to turn down the chance to play for a 15A team? (At the time Bath Rangers would have been a 15E team.)

I decided, much to the disappointment of my dad, let it be said, to join Cherry Orchard and it was the best decision I ever made. Dad actually said to me, 'you're an awful man for what you are doing'. He was a quiet, shy and loyal man who worked at the old Jefferson Smurfit paper mill. I remember he would leave for work at 6.30am and with him would be his trusty bike. That bike was like a friend, he never cycled it to work mind, he used to walk the bike to work. That bike was kept in great condition and was polished for hours; he loved it. On his way back from work in the evening he would walk it home and then cycle it for the last mile. We used to give him an awful slagging for it.

My decision to join Cherry Orchard, without discussing it with him, had left a sour feeling with him. I did not think he would come up to my first game but he was there. I remember we won 7–0 and I scored twice. On the way home he said 'that's a great team'. That was it, nothing more. My dad never really gave me praise directly; he would tell my mother when I had a good game and she would tell me later what he said, that was his way really.

If I done something bad on the pitch he would let me know, he did not like it when a player got carded or fouled another player and he especially did not like it if I did it.

He hated me getting booked, I would sometimes lose my temper in a game and when I did he would be sure to let me know. But he came to every match I played in and really supported me. He was quite strict with me, I remember other kids around Ringsend would stay out till 9.00 – 9.30 whereas I had to be in by 7.30 every evening. He had my interests at heart though.

That Cherry Orchard team was one of the best sides I was ever involved in; we went unbeaten that season, winning the League and both Cups. We had some great players in that team; Christy Bradley, Jackie Jameson and Tony Maher.

Christy and Jackie were unbelievable footballers, they could have played at the highest level, but they had a bit of an attitude about them though. They knew they were good and could turn it on and sometimes they could not be bothered. John Wilkes used to go mad with them, they had so much ability. I know Jackie played League of Ireland and had a great career but he could have made it in England, he was that good.

I remember being really upset when John Wilkes rang me to tell me that Jackie had passed away. It was a real shame because he was such a lovely lad and I got on very well with him, my father had great time for him and thought he was our best player. I missed his funeral but made a point of getting home later in the year and travelled down with Gerry Flynn to visit his grave and pay my respects.

Tony Maher was a great player and actually came over for a trial at the same time as I did with Derby County.

He was a great full-back similar to Denis Irwin, he just got on with the job. I remember that Tony played really well over the two week trial, better than me actually but they must have seen something in me as they picked me.

That was my third trial in England and it was a case of third time lucky as I thought I had missed my chance to be honest. My first trial in England came for arguably the biggest club in England, Manchester United. I was lucky enough to have been spotted by the legendary Billy Behan who took me over to Manchester United for a trial. He came down to the house to speak with my Ma and Da, Billy explained that I would be well looked after and I would be safe. My Ma didn't want me to go but my Da was ok with it.

There were two other players that went on the trial with me and who would later go on to become two of the biggest names in Irish soccer history, they were none other than Frank Stapleton and David O'Leary.

I had first met Frank when we were both picked for the Irish Schoolboy side, we used to meet up on Merrion Square before heading out to training. Like now, I was quiet and shy, I was playing E League football with Bath Rangers which compared to the A League players in the Schoolboy selection was like Manchester United players being picked alongside non-League players. Frank came up to me on one of my first times there and said to me, 'What's your name?' I said Dave and that was it really, we became friends easy enough.

Frank was a big fella even then and seemed more mature for his age; when we were over at Manchester he looked after me and we stayed friends ever since. I was best man at his wedding and he was best man at my first wedding.

Frank got married in Malahide and a few weeks before the wedding he asked me if I would be his best man, I was delighted and honoured. I had gotten to know Frank very well since that first training session out at Milltown. The day of his wedding, I had a few drinks to settle my nerves, nothing too hectic and then said a few words. I was a shy lad so it was tough to stand in front of everyone and talk, but I am glad I did it that day.

David O'Leary on the other hand was a quiet fella like me and I really did not get to know him until we were both in the Irish squad years later.

None of the three of us were picked. They said I was not good enough, which was fair enough but funnily enough years later United forked out £900,000 for Frank when he was at Arsenal. Imagine, they could have had him for nothing.

Billy kept working for me in the background though and also got me a trial at Birmingham City. I actually thought I had played better during the Birmingham trial than I did for the Derby trial but again they also said I was not good enough.

Like Frank with Manchester United, years later Birmingham had to pay to sign me, only not as much as United paid for Frank, they paid £350,000 to sign me.

I remember that first year I was at Derby County I lived with this Polish lady who would give us a KitKat every Sunday. I was on eight pounds a week and Derby paid for my digs, by Sunday we would not have a bob between us and would head down to some local girls we knew for 10p to get a bar of chocolate. We always paid them back when we got our wages.

In your first year as an apprentice you are given three players to look after; Roy McFarland, Archie Gemmill and Colin Todd. You had to look after their boots and make sure they were scrubbed clean and polished. As well as that you had to sweep the litter and clean the baths. The manager in charge of Derby at the time and the man who brought me to Derby was none other than Brian Clough; although it would be Colin Murphy who would give me my debut it was Clough that gave me my first impression of how a football manager should be.

Cloughie looked after his first team players and liked everything to be just right for them, if you were in charge of cleaning their boots and they were not up to scratch then he would go ballistic and come down on you like a ton of bricks.

Clough was very heavy-handed, I remember one time I was at a reserve game, I think Derby were playing against Burton Albion and I remember afterwards, Clough came into the dressing room and went around each player, stopping at five or six saying 'Guilty'. All the guilty players had to go to his office in the morning where he told them that they would not be getting new contracts and they could leave now or in the summer.

I tried to avoid getting in his way but found myself coming under his radar sooner than I thought when during one of my first weeks at the club he entrusted me with taking his two sons, Simon and Nigel; who himself would be a great player and is now the manager at Derby, to their match day seats.

He came up to me with his two sons and said to me 'Irishman (he always called me Irishman from that point on), hold my two sons' hands and take them to their seats, if you let go of their hands, I'll cut your balls off'.

I was a nervous wreck now, but grabbed their hands and headed off; we were no sooner out of sight when they got away from me and starting running. I thought to myself, 'ah jaysus, what am I going to do?' Thankfully the man at the turnstiles recognised me and let me after them and I made sure they were at their seats. On my way back Brian said to me 'Good lad Irishman, Good lad'. If he had only known!

Another time I was cleaning the changing rooms and the phone rang, it was Clough. Derby had just beaten Liverpool 2–0 and he was in great form, he said to me, 'young man, fetch me some whiskey and get your arse down here'. When I got down there with the whiskey, I noticed there was another man in the room and it was none other than the legendary Bill Shankly. Brian had just asked Bill who was the best player he had ever bought and Bill had replied, 'Ray Clemence', he then saw me and shook my hand. There I was, a 16-year-old listening to these two great men, the dream had started.

Another time we were in the changing rooms and the phone rang. Alan Lewis, a fellow apprentice, picked up the phone and Clough said 'bring me down a whiskey'.

Lewis said, 'Fuck off'.

To which an incensed Clough said, 'do you know who I am?'

Lewis, who was a bit of a character replied, 'Do you know who you are talking to?'

An increasingly agitated Clough said 'No', at which point Lewis replied, 'Well Fuck off again then', at which point we all ran for our lives. I would have loved to have been a fly on the wall in his office to see his face.

Almost all stories with Clough involve a drink, which is not a reflection of his character, it's just I suppose as a trainee I would have been in or around after a match or on the lucky occasion that one of us was picked to travel with the first team and drinking would have formed part of that experience.

There was a culture of drinking in football at that time and it was widely accepted, you could have a beer after a game and there wasn't too much made about it. I remember players often not waiting until they got home, especially after a good result away from home. One time we were playing Liverpool again and we came away with a very credible 1–1 draw, a result that left Cloughie pleased.

We were on our way back down the M6 to the East Midlands and he got the bus driver to pull in along the M6 and he sent one of the apprentices down to get a slab of beer. I was one of the lucky trainees that had been picked to travel for the game although I was not the one sent down. Anyway I am not sure who got the slab of beers out, but they were passed around the coach to the players. It might be frowned upon now but I think it was a nice gesture for the lads.

I suppose everyone has their Clough stories and I could write a separate book about him he was such a character, I remember another day we were playing six-a-side together and Clough was playing and he took a shot that rolled along the line. One of the senior players, I don't remember who, shouted 'No goal' and cleared the ball away, however, Clough claimed it was a goal and was arguing that it was with everyone; eventually he turns, points at me and says, 'Ask the Irishman'.

This is my moment to shine, and trying to be as honest as I can, I say, 'it wasn't a goal boss'. To which Clough replies, quick as you like, 'Fucking Irishman, doesn't speak for three months and then the first thing he says is a lie'.

Clough was never a man to mince his words and would dare you to speak to him about money, as apprentices we were on shit money and we were forever trying to build up the courage to go and ask for raises.

The only way to decide who would head down to his office and ask was by pulling straws, there was no one brave enough just to head down and ask, we all knew it would be a no anyway. I got lucky on a number of occasions but my time had to come to walk down the corridor to his office, I pulled the short straw and the lads were pushing me to go down. I got into his office and I remember I was shaking, and managed to stutter something that I think sounded like, 'I've come into talk to you about a raise,' to which Clough, who hadn't even looked up said, 'why don't you come back when you're sober, now fuck off'.

He was good to me though and maybe I am imagining this now and it is very easy to say when he is not around to confirm or deny the same, but I think he had a soft spot for me and wanted me to do well. Whenever he saw that I was homesick he would send me off home for a few days and that helped me settle in to life at Derby. It certainly made it easier to know that

I got to see my family and friends every now and then. One time he gave me a £10 note and told me to buy some flowers for my Ma. He said he would know if I got them or not and I would be in trouble with him if I didn't get them. I made sure I got them.

I did not spend a lot of time under Clough at Derby. The time I had, which obviously left an impression on me, was brief and within a few months of my arriving he had left the club. He was a different breath of a manager to the guys at the time and nowadays, it did not matter to him whether you were a fresh faced apprentice or a seasoned professional, he struck a remarkable mix of respect and fear into them all.

He was very strict, everyone had to have short hair and you could never be seen with your hands in your pockets. One time he saw Roy MacFarland with his hands in his pockets but said nothing about it. The following day Roy was bemused as to why his pockets were sewn shut. The laundry lady told him she had a message from the boss to do it.

By the time my second year at Derby arrived Brian had left and I had moved up to £25 a week. I had moved up the ranks and was now playing with the reserves, mind you I was still cleaning toilets and boots. The boots I was now responsible for were actually those of the new boss Dave MacKay and his assistant Des Anderson.

Dave was a great player and hard as nails on the pitch but as a manager I found him very quiet, he was a nice fellow. This was a man who broke his leg three times during his career, but off the pitch you did not see the hard person.

That said if he played in a practice match and someone tackled him unfairly then he would lose his temper, even though he himself would steam into people in training all the time.

Dave was very good to me and gave me my first taste of action with the first team.

I remember he took the Derby team to Madrid for a pre-season friendly match against Athletico. I along with the other apprentices had been left at home, however after a couple of injuries to players he put a call into the Baseball Ground to have me get my gear and come over. I had to get to the ground, get my kit and boots and fly over on my own. I was then collected from the airport.

Dave said I would not play any part but was there just in case, however 10 minutes into the second half he gave me my first start with the first team in a Derby shirt. It was an amazing feeling, even though it was a friendly the stadium was packed and the adrenalin rush I got from that was unreal. The minute I heard the roar of the fans the nerves went away.

I made the bench for a game against Middlesbrough but did not make it on to the field of play. It was the only time that season that I got near to making my first team competitive debut.

Despite having been signed by Brian Clough and managed by Dave MacKay I actually made my first start for Derby under Colin Murphy.

I was in the reserve team playing in the Central League when I was called into the team for the game against Leeds. I will never forget it, it was 12 February 1977, a ticket to the game would have cost £1.80 imagine, and we lost 1–0. Derby had a severe injury crisis before the game, it was like a blood bath; we had some players out and Colin pulled me aside and told me that the way things were going I could be involved on Saturday.

The day of the game, it bucketed down with rain and I genuinely thought the game would be called off it was so bad, I actually prayed that it would, I had spent the previous night tossing and turning in bed with worry. However, they did a pitch inspection and it got the go ahead and then at 2pm I saw the team sheet and realised I was playing. Andy Gray was the Leeds winger at the time that I should have been marking and he was a class player, thankfully he was missing that night, because who knows what would have happened then. But he was ruled out and I marked my Derby debut with the man of the match award.

As I said I had played most of my football in midfield but Colin moved me to right-back for that game and that was where I would make my name.

Once I got into the Derby side there was no stopping me it seemed, I finished the season in the team with 23 appearances in all competitions. I was now a converted right-back it seemed and the decision by Murphy seemed to be paying off although I did manage to return to midfield for one last swansong that was near the end of the season when we drew 0–0 with Arsenal at Highbury. I didn't do enough to stay there and was back in my full-back position for the next game at West Ham.

It's funny how things turned around for me in a short space of time at Derby, in the weeks coming up to my first team debut I was probably at my lowest ebb in my all too brief English football career.

I had not played a game in six weeks due to a mixture of bad weather and injury and was genuinely starting to think I would never make it in English football. Murphy had already decided that he did not rate me as a midfielder, I was worried that he did not rate me as a player, as I know he had concerns about my temperament and ability to show passion, although it turns out he needn't have worried. He had moved me to right-back for a reserve game against Everton, where I had a nightmare against a fella by the name of Ronnie Goodlass. It just seemed that nothing was going right. I was ready to throw in the towel and head home. I was really fed up, a lot of it had to do with where I was living, which was in Coventry.

One of the things that helped me settle better was moving into digs in Aston-on-Trent with Mr and Mrs Dave Emsley. I had been living with a girl, Barbara Weston, who was my first girlfriend; I had met her at a football match and got chatting to her and before long we were together. I was only 17 or 18 when I met her and soon enough we were living together in a flat. But it did not work out at all, it was never going to, we were only kids and the situation soon started to affect my footballing life. In the end, we broke up and I moved in with the Emsleys where I was happy as a sandboy with them, they were lovely people and they treated me like I was their son. They already had a six-year-old boy and I used to get on so well with him. They were great for me, I loved living there and I remember I used to help out around the house, I actually don't think I would have made it in England without them.

In the end I settled down and despite Murphy having plenty of options at right-back for the Leeds game he ended up picking me and I will never forget him for that.

In my second game for Derby I had to mark Steve Heighway, it was some introduction to League football, my debut at home to Leeds and then my second game at Anfield against Liverpool, marking one of the best wingers in the game. We lost 3–1 but I thought I had done well against Steve. That first 12 months in the Derby team was a whirlwind, so much praise came my way it was hard to keep my feet on the ground, and I remember having to mark the great Peter Barnes and getting the man of the match award, setting up a goal in a 2–1 win. I remember Kenny Dalglish naming me in his XI of opponents who had caught his eye. Although I don't think he passed on that list to Bob Paisley as they never made an offer for me! I was also named the Shoot magazine right-back of the year, all this and I was still only 19.

Colin was a good coach but he was not a great manager, I am grateful to him for giving me my debut and converting me to a right-back but truth be told I never really took to him. I often felt that Colin picked on me especially as I was shy and an easy target. He would often bawl me out. He definitely gave me more bollockings than anyone else, although that said I think I made it easy for him as I used to be too scared to speak up and just kept quiet.

That said I must have done something right that night of my debut because it would be 91 games before I would miss another League match. When I came into the side we were struggling for results and were in danger of dropping down to Division Two. My arrival in the side coincided with a change of fortune although I think the signing of Gerry Daly, from Manchester United, had more to do with it.

Daly was an amazing player and had a good scoring record for a midfielder. That season we ended staying up, finishing 15th in the table, thanks to a run of just two defeats in 17 games, it was a stunning end to the season. To show just how tight it was and how lucky we were, we finished seven places and just four points above Spurs who finished bottom and were relegated and did not win any games away from home that season.

My 92nd consecutive game in the side was meant to be against Arsenal who back then played at Highbury, however the previous game against Manchester United at home I had been sent off, my first red card and sending off in top flight English football, and my incredible run was coming to an end.

In fact that was my first sending off ever, I had been booked before mainly for minor infringements but have never seen red and I was not a dirty player at all. I was sent off for a tackle on the great Mickey Thomas, I had been booked before that though, so I supposed I had to go under the laws of the game but there had been a lot of hard tackles going in that night, far worse than what I had done, I remember one tackle sent Billy Caskey flying into the wall at the side of the pitch.

When I made the first team at Derby one of the major things people noticed about me was my range of passing and how I could find a player with a 30–35 yard ball. I can tell you that this was not something that came naturally to me, being honest when I first came to Derby, my passing was absolutely shocking. I had to really work on it and I used to spend time after training with one of the younger lads, just hitting long ball after long ball and from all sorts of angles. Eventually I began to get them right and they started to land right on the player's foot but it took a lot of practice.

One of the things that helped me develop as right-back was the fact that I would always get stuck into a winger early on to let him know I was there. Wingers were a different breed from your central midfielders and forwards, they did not like me getting in their faces straight away, that is why a lot of managers did not use them a lot, they preferred their players to get stuck in.

Despite being considered too slow for midfield I seemed suited to the role of right-back and while Murphy spotted my potential as a full-back, a lot of my conversion must go to Steve Powell. Like me, Steve had come through the ranks to the first team, in fact we were the first players in eight years to make the breakthrough from the youth team to the senior side and manage to stay there, a few lads progressed but they generally moved on after a while.

While I was an outsider in Derby, Powell was Derby through and through, he had been born in the area and his dad had also played for the club. Steve would go on to spend his whole career with the Rams. He was also a good player and one of the things he helped me do was to make myself faster. You would think it would be all about running but he actually told me it was about the stomach and gave me some exercises that helped me. They actually helped my breathing, whereas before I was knackered after running up the wing and would struggle to get back, after the exercises I was able to run up and down no problem, although I still looked knackered, Steve had no tips for that.

The other players at the club also played a large part, and they really took me in as one of their own right from the start. I met some great lads at Derby. The likes of Colin Todd, Charlie George and Roy McFarland were not just great players, they were great guys to know too. I got to know Todd very well, like me he liked to gamble and we became good auld pals, I actually played with him at Birmingham, he was one of the reasons I went there.

I thought Charlie George was one of the best players I ever played with and to me he is quite a legend of the game, especially for all that he achieved with Arsenal. Despite being a shy lad who kept to myself I actually got on well with all the lads, they all really took me in as one of their own and made me feel part of the team.

When I look back and think of games that stand out for me, games where I came off the pitch, not only pleased that I had given 100 per cent but also felt that I had done more than that, one that stands out is when I was with Derby and we beat Brian Clough's Nottingham Forest 4-1 at home.

That night I was marking John Robertson, the former Scottish international, who at the time was one of the best wingers in England. I had done my homework on him and asked around the players to get an insight into him. I knew he liked to cut inside and then out. I stuck tight to him the whole 90 minutes making sure that he did not get any time on the ball. Although I have to admit, that while I had done my homework and played well, I was ably assisted by Leighton James that night, he had a great game.

A couple of years later when I was a regular in the first team at Derby I crossed paths with the great Bill Shankly once again. By now he had left Liverpool and was out of the game. We were playing Everton in the quarter-final of the FA Cup at Goodison and in preparation for the game we were staying at a hotel in Stockport and who comes into see us, only Bill Shankly. As has been well documented over the years Bill disliked Everton with a passion and he wanted to help us so he came to have lunch with Colin Murphy and Donald O'Riordan.

He had placed a call with the club to find out where we were staying, I was lucky enough to be invited along to the lunch. Bill told me that the Everton left-back on the day was rubbish and that the whole team was rubbish. He spent five hours with us that day and all he talked about was Liverpool. Even though he was no longer manager you could tell how much he really loved that club.

Unfortunately we lost 2–0 that day although Liverpool would beat Everton 3–0 in a replay in the semi-finals, so I imagine Mr Shankly would have been happy with that.

Another time we played West Brom and Willy Johnson their winger had a great game, he gave me the go around that day. Like every other time I have a bad game I was feeling down and the first person I bumped into was Bill Shankly. He asked me how I was feeling, and I said 'Rubbish' and he replied to me 'that's because you are not fit son'. We had not played in a few weeks due to the weather so I would not have been match fit but Bill had a way of seeing these things.

In my six years at Derby I played under five different managers, I was signed by Clough, made my debut under Murphy and was sold by Addison, in between there was Dave McKay and Tommy Docherty.

Tommy arrived at Derby under a bit of a cloud as he had been sacked by Manchester United after it became public that he had had an affair with Mary Brown, who was the wife of one of the physiotherapists at the club at the time. Tommy had left his wife to be with Mary and it was a big controversy at the time. The Manchester United board obviously had their values as they sacked him for a breach of contract despite Tommy leading them to the FA Cup over Liverpool a few months before. I don't think you would see that nowadays so you have to admire the way Manchester United acted at the time.

Derby had no such issues and they appointed him as manager in September after they had sacked Murphy. Tommy was a good manager and he was very good to me and for my career. He was always talking me up to the press and spoke highly of me which was good to hear, he used to tell everyone who would listen that I was the best young right-back in England and if I was English the press would be extolling me.

He was very fair to me too, I think he knew I was young and he let me off once or twice when maybe he should have been stricter. I remember one time we were heading away on a trip abroad and I let him down by not turning up to go and he fined me two weeks' wages.

He then took pity on me and instead he just gave a fine of two quid and told me to tell everyone it was two weeks. He knew that I had no money and tried to help me out. He said the way I played I would be dead by 25. There was nothing malicious in his comment to me, I think he was just on about how determined and how much I got stuck in. The funny thing is that in a strange way he was right.

When Tommy first came in, he made an immediate impact and we played brilliantly but he started selling players to raise money and the players he brought in were not as good. In the end we fell away and were crap to be honest.

Tommy was a good character outside of football, he was always cracking jokes, every time he saw me, Gerry Daly or any of the other Irish lads at Derby at the time, he loved to say, 'how is yer man' the way we say it in Dublin.

In the end he was sacked as results were not good enough and we were playing rubbish, he had to go. To his credit he wanted to play attacking football which suited me. I don't think he had the best of relationships with some of the players, I know him and Gerry Daly did not get on too well and really if you are to succeed at a club you need to have the players on your side.

The Doc as he was known was gone and while he might have been a big name, the Derby board went the opposite way for his replacement, the little known Colin Addison. Addison had made a name for himself as a player manager with Hereford and also managed in South Africa and Newport before taking on an assistant manager role with WBA.

I think his appointment at the time was a shock to a few people around the club but in true player fashion you have to support the decision and give the new man a chance. Sadly for me his appointment would signal the end of my time in the white of Derby not to mention the club's status as a top division side.

Sometimes it seems like I always try to remember the bad times but there were plenty of good times, my breakthrough to the first team for one, my debut for Ireland and also my first goal in English football which came under Addison.

I actually scored my first goal for Derby in a pre-season friendly against Dutch side Nijmegen but it would be a while before I grabbed my first League goal. I thought I had scored it when we played Norwich early on in the 1977–78 season but it was ruled out as Kevin Hector was offside and it would be another season before I actually broke my duck in English football.

It was at the start of the season and I remember we were playing Arsenal at home and went two nil down. Addison went ballistic with us at half-time, and rightly so, we had been poor in the first half and Arsenal was the better side. However, we came out the second half determined and went on to win the game 3–2 with me getting my first ever goal and a sweet one at that.

We had won a corner and it was taken, I cannot remember by whom, but anyway it was headed clear by an Arsenal defender and I just hit first time and it flew right into the top corner. What a way to score your first goal in English football and past the legendary Pat Jennings as well.

Sadly my time at Derby did not end the way it should have. I spent six great years at the club and had developed as a footballer there and made my Ireland debut while I was there so I had and still have very fond memories of my time with the club.

I did not handle my departure from the club very well, I had heard snippets of rumours, nothing official, that Manchester United, Aston Villa, Coventry and Birmingham were interested in me and it turned my head a bit. I was flattered and shocked that Dave Sexton, the Man United manager was interested in me; it was a good confidence booster, although it was just rumours and nothing ever happened in the end.

But Derby was on a downward spiral under Addison at the time and heading for Division Two. I had played all my football in Division One and wanted to remain at the top for as long as I could.

I remember we were playing away to Bristol City in the FA Cup and the night before the game I went in the office to meet with Addison. His assistant John Newman was with him but that did not put me off, I wanted to know what was going on so I asked them outright to be honest with me and tell me if any club had come in for me.

Addison told me no straight away and then looked at Newman who also said no, I should have left it at that but I did not believe them and instead of keeping my mouth shut I asked Addison not to play me on the Saturday as I did not want to be Cup tied ahead of any move from the club; he refused my request and told me to be on the coach heading to the game and to report for team duty.

I had decided at that point that I would go, however, on my way to the ground to meet the players I had a change of mind, my head was wrecked so I took a drive up to the Derbyshire hillsides to clear my head and decide what to do. The team eventually left without me, and it got to the papers, one paper went with the headline 'Rebel without a cause'.

I thought about it all day and eventually decided to head down on the train to the team hotel that evening, I remember Bruce Rioch came and met me when I got there. The two of us headed to the hotel where the team was staying but when I got there Addison would not talk to me and I was told to go to bed.

The follow morning he tore into me and told me I was a disgrace to the club and to pack my bags and to head back to Derby. He also fined me two weeks' wages and I was suspended. Rioch stood up for me in the dressing room, and said he felt that harsh. Addison turned to him and said you can shut up too because you are heading back with him.

I remember the two of us heading up to the train station and Rioch said to me, 'Are you ok for money?' I told him I was not, I was screwed, I had just been fined £300 by the manager, it was a lot of money. He gave me £100 to help me out; it was a very nice gesture by him and a lot of money in those days. I actually never paid him back would you know, it is something that I have to carry with me. He had my back that day though; he was not the only one though, a few players were on my side although Bruce was definitely the loudest.

I handed in a written request shortly after, which effectively cost me about £5,000 but I did not care at the time though as I wanted to leave.

I remember Gordon Milne, who was manager at Coventry at the time and one of the clubs supposedly interested in me, came out shortly afterwards giving out about my attitude. I thought it was a very unfair thing to do, he did not know me. People should not say things about people or situations they don't know anything about. I had never met him; I knew nothing about him yet here he was speaking about my attitude.

I admit I had been young and stupid with the way I had acted but if you ask any manager I played under and they will tell you I had a good attitude.

That said I did have a few minor rows with Addison, we were never the same again after the Bristol City incident. Five days after the clash in Bristol, Addison called me into his office for a chat and told me I was due to face Manchester United at the weekend, I had trained on my own all week but now suddenly I was being told that I was back in the team. A week earlier I had been banned from the training ground and fined two weeks' wages, now here I was being told I was back in the team.

I did not know what to think of it all, I asked him about my wages and that I wanted them but I was told where to go on that one.

We lost that Saturday against United, going down 3–1, however, the reception I got from the fans was fantastic, I was worried how they would react to me, I thought they would slaughter me but they did not. I was a fans' favourite at the time and instead of turning against me they sided with me, it was a great boost and made my decision to want to leave even harder. They knew the club needed the money for me though and felt in some shape or form that I was doing the right thing, even if I was going about it arseways.

Addison had another go at me on television afterwards; that was a mad thing to do and a tad inexperienced on his behalf. It did not help relations between us at any rate and at the end of the season when our relegation was confirmed I knew I would be leaving.

I remember when I finally did leave in the summer he called me at my home and told me to come into the club in the morning, that he wanted to have a chat with me.

I went in next day and he said to me that Birmingham City had come and made an offer for me and was I interested? I said they had just been promoted and we were in Division Two so yes I was interested. He then just said, 'Don't ask for phone numbers when you talk to them'.

That meant I was not to ask for astronomical wages, in those days you did not have an agent like you have today, so you went down by yourself and met the manager and you decided if you wanted to go or not. Which is what I did, I went down and met Jim Smith and within 10 minutes I was back in Division One with Birmingham City. Jim told me he would pay me the same money as I was on at Derby, which was £200 week, with a £50 performance bonus on top of it for every game I played.

I was sad to be leaving Derby, I had a great relationship with the fans and had enjoyed my time at the club but Addison himself admitted that he needed to sell me to help rebuild the side and the money they got from Birmingham, which was a club record at the time for the Brum, helped him to build in positions he needed to.

I remember I went in to get my boots the following day and there was a queue of fans buying their season ticket for the new season. One of them came over to me and said he could not wait for the new season as with the likes of players like me at the club Derby were going to go straight back up.

I did not have the heart to tell him I was leaving, he would have probably read about it in the papers the next day.

A Derby teammate recalls Dave: Don O'Riordan

Don O'Riordan shared digs with Dave in Derby and he recalls the then 15-year-old as an easy going and quiet guy.

'I first came across Dave Langan when we were both involved with the Dublin Schoolboys Under-15 team. That side and the Ireland national Under-15 side was mainly made up of players from Cherry Orchard and Home Farm as they were the top two teams at that level at the time.

'You could see then that Dave was a good player and was going to make it in the game. It's funny but before we would eventually share digs at Derby, Dave was actually my replacement at Cherry Orchard.

'When it emerged that I would be heading off to Derby County in that summer of 1972, John Wilkes and Gerry Flynn the managers of Cherry Orchard had seen my replacement in Dave, who was with Bath Rangers at the time and looked to sign him for the Orchard.

'He had gone to Manchester United just before that for a trial but didn't get an offer and both John and Gerry told him if he joined the Orchard he would get another chance across the water and they were right.

'I remember when I was back in Dublin for a visit in my first year I went to see the Orchard play and Dave was incredible that day. I knew he was good but that day he was on a different level to everyone else and played with such energy and showed great ability I knew he would soon get a chance to go to England. As promised John got him a trial at Derby, it didn't take the coaches long to see he was a very good player and they signed him in the summer of 1973.

'When he arrived at the training ground he was this shy dark-haired Irish kid who would only speak when spoken to, I reckon every one of the apprentices thought "this guy will struggle" but once Dave crossed the white line he was a different animal.

'I think one of the things that helped Dave settle so well in life at Derby was the fact that there was a strong Irish contingent there at the time as Eddie Hogan and Tony Buckley who had also played on the Ireland Under-15 team were there.

'We lived with a Polish couple, Mr and Mrs Slovinski and their kids in a huge house; there was the four of us Irish lads and three English lads in the house.

'In those days Dave and I were not really lads who went out too often, we couldn't afford to I suppose and of course we were quite dedicated. We were both seeing girls and most of the time we would go to see them and get back to the digs before 10.30pm.

'The lads at the club would give us a ribbing for being under the thumb and not going out but we accepted it and it's funny that most of those lads that teased us never got a professional contract at 18 but we did, so being boring must have paid off.

'Because Dave and I were so close back then there would have been times when I would see him get down about something. It might be because he didn't get a game in the reserves, which he used to take very hard or he might have had an argument with his girlfriend.

'Each time something happened he would state that he had enough and was going back home. I heard it dozens of times although he never said it to anyone else only me. I think though we both knew we were lucky to be where we were and knew hundreds, maybe thousands of lads back home would have loved to have been in our shoes. When one was down complaining to the other we would try to help by reminding each other about this, although there were times when it was very difficult to get through to him.

'Sometimes he would get down over something and wouldn't divulge why and no matter what I'd say to him he would refuse to talk about it. Again it might have been a girlfriend argument or a letter with bad news from home and I would try to encourage him to break down the wall he was hiding behind.

'It was never worrying but sometimes frustrating but we all handle disappointment in different ways?

'As time went on he settled into the Reserve team but as expected for a young lad playing at a decent level he didn't boss the game as he had back in Dublin playing for the Orchard against St Kevin's Boys. His effect on the game was carrying less weight because he was playing against players who were as good as him but usually older and stronger and so he was almost stuck in a rut playing in the Reserves but not perhaps improving as expected.

'He had energy in abundance, a decent striker of the ball, had pace and was a winner, but to play on the first team in a midfield role would require a little more of something and he probably was frustrated at that stage.

'I can't remember exactly what happened but I recall Colin Murphy being involved in the decision to play Dave at right-back and he was superb. After his second game playing there people saw that the first brilliant performance was no fluke and as it happened he took to the position like the proverbial "duck". He was outstanding at times in big games against big time teams and players but he never showed any nerves and played like I'd seen him play when I first returned to Dublin to see him play for the Orchard. He never looked back after that.

'There is a great story from our training sessions that has probably never been told before, in those days all the apprentices got there before 9am with the first team starting training at 10.30am. The apprentice's job was to get the players' (professionals) kit out on their seats with their polished boots under their seat ready for their arrival.

'Once that was done we would rush out to an area where there was a goal and a sand pit where the keepers trained and we would play out the Kevin Keegan and John Toshack roles with Dave providing running commentary. Dave was brilliant at it and sounded like he was on the BBC covering a game.

'I remember at first we would get shouted at by the coaches because we never warmed up we just went into blasting balls from all angles into the empty net literally from 9.15 till 10.30am till the warm up for training started. This went on for about two weeks with just us involved but soon some of the other apprentices and young pros would join in and eventually we had first team players involved with the same commentary being delivered by Dave.

'The great Charlie George began to join in this game and there were often up to 20 players waiting for Dave or myself to deliver a cross that would get Dave's commentary treatment.

'Charlie loved to hear Dave commentating, it was brilliant just like we did as kids on the street in Ballyfermot or in Ringsend and here was Charlie George already a superstar joining in and not bothered that Dave was calling him by another superstar's name.

'We had great fun though I remember another time we were away with Ireland Under-18s for a tournament in Monte Carlo. After the final game, we were allowed to go out for a few beers and ended up all the worst for it. Dave and I in particular were a bit rough and felt like getting sick but the other lad we were sharing with told us not to get sick in the bathroom so we both stood on the balcony and vomited, you could hear the sick smacking the pavement four floors below us. We were never proud of that incident in such a historical city.

'Dave then collapsed onto the bed and there was no waking him. The rest of the lads in the team were back in the hotel up to no good. We had all gathered in our room, although not even that noise could wake Dave. Every room had a wake-up call for 5.15am and we all knew that we would be left behind if we failed to show for the 6am bus to the airport. The lads plotted a trick and moved the other players' luggage and mine to their rooms and left Dave sleeping off his hangover.

'At 2.30am everyone in the squad gathered in the lobby and persuaded the receptionist to call our room and wake Dave telling him to get his arse down to the bus as it was now 5.55am and he had only five minutes to catch a ride. We all pulled up chairs and place them in front of the elevator waiting for the doors to open.

'What emerged was a half dressed and dishevelled Dave Langan in a state, his case was not closed properly and all his stuff was hanging out. We all stood and clapped him but he failed to realise the joke. He was a little shocked but wanted us to hurry up and get our stuff because the bus was about to leave. We were rolling around on the floor with laughter. We eventually pointed out it was still dark outside and to check his watch at which point he realised he had been tricked and disappeared back into the lift muttering a few swear words.'

Chapter Three

Me and Mandy

My first wife, Mandy Hallam was actually the niece of Derby skipper Roy McFarland and was from the Derby area. She would have been around the ground at the time, so I would have known who she was and who she was related to. She actually worked as a civil servant with the Department of Health and Social Services.

This one time she was up at the club and we happened to get chatting, I asked her to go for a drink. I cannot remember where we went for the drink but I do remember that we really clicked that night, from there everything moved very fast and we were married within the year, expecting our first child. We got married on 4 September 1978 at Saint Mary's Roman Catholic Church in Derby. It was a Monday. I was only 22 and she was 21, it was a lot to take in and all very sudden. Roy was fine about us getting together and the wedding itself was a big one. I remember Frank Stapleton repaid the favour and was best man for me. There was a lovely picture in the Derby Telegraph at the time, it showed me, Mandy and Frank in it. Frank was planting a kiss on the cheek of Mandy in the picture. It was a lovely day and my family came over for it, I remember my youngster sister Audrey, who was only 15 at the time, getting a dance off Charlie George, who was a bit of a heart throb at the time.

I think when I look back now that I caused Mandy a lot of heartache, we were too young for it all and I don't think I was good for her at all. Everything happened very fast, the courtship and the marriage and it was not long before we had a child. My first son Elliot was born shortly after we got married, I might not have been the best father and certainly would not claim any father of the year award but I will never forget the day he was born. It was an immense feeling, like there was a warm glow around me, although my heart was in my mouth when he first came out. The nurses and doctors had to use forceps to get him out and he did not cry straight away. They gave him a smack on the bum and that got him going.

Being a father was very overwhelming though.

Shortly after Elliot was born I was transferred to Birmingham and that only seemed to make things more difficult, we had to move down there to be near the club and that was hard for Mandy and the baby who did not know anyone in Birmingham and was away from her family.

I was not making the effort I should have been and was out a lot in those days, partying and drinking and not facing up to my duties. Eventually we split up and she moved back to Derby. I sold the house we had been living in to help set them up and I moved into a place that Phil Hawker had owned. I was only seeing Elliot in midweek or the odd weekend now and again, it was not an ideal situation for any of us. Elliot was missing out on having a father.

I think neither one of us was ready for the responsibility but Mandy was a nice girl and deserved better. She brought up Elliot very well. My game was suffering as well because my personal life was in such turmoil and I remember Jim Smith telling me to get my head right as I was not playing well at all. Eventually I went from not playing well to getting badly injured and that was too much pressure for all of us.

I do wish I was a lot closer to Elliot and I have to take the blame for that, I didn't make the best effort especially when I got injured and I was on crutches. I could not drive at that point and went off the rails. I was depressed and drinking heavily, the hardest thing about being injured is that everybody forgets you, the management team do not want to see you as you are no good to them while you are not involved in training, you lose contact with the players a bit. It was hard but I found it harder as all I ever wanted to do was play football, nothing else mattered.

I was in a bad way, out of the game I loved, living in a rented house while my wife and child lived in Derby. I could not think straight and slipped into depression, and it was easy to start drinking and not face up to my responsibilities.

I remember the first time I thought that drink was going to be a good answer, I was in the treatment room and they were taking the stitches out, the doctor told me that I would be on crutches for six to eight weeks. I was devastated. I was walking out and met Mick Ferguson, who was a centre-forward who had initially joined us on loan from Everton. Mick asked if I wanted to head to the pub with him and it was an easy decision to say yes.

We spent the whole day in the pub and got blotto, I was buying drinks for people I did not know and had never met. Because the knee was so bad and career-threatening, the Physiotherapist said they could not start work on it for a number of weeks so I had nothing to do. I was renting off Phil Hawker, who was a young left-back at the club at the time and there was a pub called the Woodman just a quarter of a mile down the road, every day I headed down there on my crutches, sat in the corner and drank. It's funny but when you have a few bob in your pocket everyone wants to know you, I became a regular and everyone knew me, especially as I was often buying them drinks. Come closing time the owner of the Woodman would drive me home with loads of wine and I used to sit in the sitting room and finish them off too. I was in a bad place in my head and I would often sit on my own with my wine sobbing uncontrollably.

After a few weeks I got to go down to the club to begin work on the knee but even that was not enough for me and I kept drinking. At this point I was not making the trips to Derby so I was not seeing Mandy or Elliot. I wanted them to move down but they were not happy to move to Birmingham, she did not feel right about it and being honest we had drifted a bit by that time and both knew that it was not going to work out.

I was on a downward spiral, my personal life had fallen apart and my footballing life was no better. In the end it was a Birmingham fan that would help me to get back on my feet again. That fan was Gordon Powers. Gordon was a big football fan as well as a massive Birmingham fan and was always down at the club. He was popular with everyone there, the lads used to call him Gorytus after a horse we had won a bet on.

He came up to see me and must have been aware of my behaviour or he must have noticed my appearance, either way he called up to the house to check on me and found me drunk. He decided to take matters into his own hands and took me home with him to meet his wife Margaret, who cooked me a lovely roast dinner. It actually became a habit whereby Margaret would cook a roast dinner on a Sunday and Gordon would bring it down to me on a tray.

One day Gordon came down and found me lying in the sitting room with a load of empty wine bottles around me, he said to me, 'You're going to kill yourself'. I had met a girl called Dawn at that point and much as I had made Mandy's life hell I did the same with Dawn.

Despite my heavy drinking I was still doing my gym work trying to get my knee in shape and during one of the sessions I felt a sharp pain shoot through my back. I was in absolute agony and went to the club doctor who said there was nothing wrong. They thought it was all in my head, but the pain was so bad I persisted and eventually they sent me to the specialist who confirmed what would turn out to be my worst nightmare, I had cracked a vertebra.

I don't remember too much of the first time I went under the surgeon's knife, being honest I can not even remember too much of the build-up or the operation itself as I was under anaesthetic, however I will never forget the feeling when I came around.

There were tubes all around my knee and I did not know what was worse, the pain in my knee or in my back. It was horrendous, I did not think I would live with the pain.

The surgeon told me he had removed some cartilage and that he had found an ulcer as well when they opened up my knee. He had to remove that from the bone and, if all that wasn't bad enough, he had to put some bone marrow in and around my knee. I just went 'Oh Jesus', I could not understand it all and it was all too much to take in.

Then he told me the news that really I should have been expecting, but in all honesty I was not; the surgeon told me that I would be out of football for eight months and would require another operation, this time on my back. I could not believe it, I knew that what I had gone through was serious and I knew I would be out of football but I had never put a number on it. It was hard to take.

The second operation was two months after the knee operation, they basically opened up my hip and took out some bone marrow and filled in the crack in my back, it was called a spinal fusion.

My world was now falling apart. As well as having my knee in plaster I now had my stomach in plaster. I was miserable to be around, I was drinking, depressed and I would row with anyone that wanted to, but it was mainly Dawn, the girl who had taken over from Mandy, I was rowing with and eventually we broke up.

It was all my fault once more, all I wanted to do was to play football and when I could not it tormented me to the point that I made other people's lives a misery. I had lost my head and did not want to be there; did not want to be anywhere.

My mother and Audrey came over for the first back operation and it was good to have them over as it distracted me. Afterwards I had to wear a steel black corset with two bolts in my back, it was done to make sure that everything fused together as it should and it worked. Four or five months later they took the bolts out and that was my second back operation.

It was hard being at home, I could not fly and my mother had gone home at this stage. I rang my mother and told her that everything, as it always was, was ok and not to worry. But I was worried, not being able to do anything especially play football was a nightmare but I hated the thought of her worrying about me and if she had known what I was going through it would have killed her.

I realised though I had to get my life back on track and thankfully Gordon and Margaret were there for me once more, I am so thankful for them and their patience with me. They could have turned their back on me but they did not. The move down came because Gordon had called up to see if I was all right and I was drunk in the living room, it was during the day, and when I saw him I just started sobbing. He took pity on me and asked me if I would move in with them for a while to get myself back in order.

Before we finalised the move down, Gordon said to me in no uncertain terms, 'If you come to my house and you disrespect my wife then I'll kick you out'. I was shocked, what kind of person had I become or did he think I was?

I told him, 'I would never do that'.

The move was great, Gordon would not let me have a drink in the house and I got in the routine of going to bed early and getting myself back on track.

My dad never travelled over to England, the furthest he would go was to Ballyfermot to see his mother; he actually never saw me play in England. I asked him over a few times but he declined, he did not like the attention and the focus being on him. I remember one time hearing a story about how he was in his local pub having two pints on a Sunday when a guy came up to him and said, 'I saw your Dave on Match of the Day'. My father mumbled something and pretended to go to the bathroom but just left the bar and the full pint behind him.

I never understood that about him, he was as proud as punch of me playing in England but he hated any attention it brought him. Whenever I played for Ireland he would always go, it was funny my dad would go the game while my mother would sit at home with her rosary beads and pray for me.

My sisters and dad kept a scrapbook and even when dad died, my sisters kept it up, it contained all of the games I played that made the paper, from when I was a youngster up to playing in England.

An old friend: Paddy Murtagh

Paddy Murtagh grew up with Dave and saw him go from being a young boy playing football up by the Dodder to marrying the niece of one of the biggest footballers in England at the time.

'My relationship with Dave stretches right back to when we were young kids growing up. We would play football down by the River Dodder with one of the really old footballs that had the leather laces in them, it was that long ago!

'Growing up you could see that Dave had a talent even at that stage. He was a good thinker, a strong player on the pitch and played as if he had a bee in his bonnet. He was nonstop, all action and it was those attributes that got him to England.

'Going over to England was the best and worst move Dave ever made. It was good in the sense that he got the chance to play football at a high level, a level that he deserved to play at. However, Dave wasn't ready mentally to go over to England.

'Back in those days young footballers had no life whatsoever. The only day they had off would be a Sunday. You were always on call 24/7. It was no way to lead a life. Young guys, particularly when coming over from Ireland, weren't streetwise enough.

'They were bossed around and had no say in any matters on or off the pitch. Gerry Daly and Gerry Ryan were there at the time and they tried to look out for Dave. While Dave's parents did an excellent job in raising him Dave still had a lot to learn when he went over to England.

'Dave is essentially a shy guy. He would never be the centre of attention, that just wasn't him. When he went over to England he was very naive and was taken advantage of on occasions. Dave wouldn't stand up for himself and was sometimes walked on.

'He tried hard to be himself but given his status it was hard. I remember his first marriage to Mandy, which in my opinion wasn't the right decision for either one of them at that time; they were too young for marriage. Now Mandy is a nice girl but I don't think that she and Dave were suited to each other.

'I remember I was at the wedding and tried myself to talk Dave out of the wedding, I didn't think he was ready but he insisted he loved her and wanted to go through with it. I had to respect his decision although I don't think it helped matters that Mandy's uncle was Roy McFarland, who was one of the big names in the Derby team at that time.

'The marriage didn't last long and sadly it was a shocking position for Dave to be in, a young man making his way in England with a young baby and an estranged wife, it was a situation I hated to see him in.

'Dave ensured that Mandy was looked after when they split and he handed over everything to her, which just shows you what kind of guy Dave was. He tried to do the right thing by his son and I am sure the traditional side of Dave would have been disappointed at the breakdown of the marriage. On more than one occasion I pulled Dave aside and told him to get a grip and stop it.

'Despite his personal life being in disarray Dave's on field career continued to flourish. When he was capped for Ireland it was a moment that I'll never forget. Playing for Ireland meant everything to Dave. While playing for Derby, Birmingham and Oxford meant a great deal to Dave nothing mattered more to him than pulling on that green jersey.

His commitment to the Ireland jersey and everything that went with it stood out to me more than anything else. That's why I could never understand why Dave didn't make the Euro '88 squad.

'To me Dave got the biggest raw deal from the FAI in history. He was just cast aside and thrown on the scrap heap. You wouldn't mind if Dave had messed up on the field but I cannot remember one time that Dave let down Ireland.

'If the fans were allowed a say in the matter Dave would have been the first player in that squad. Every fan idolised Dave for the commitment and honesty of effort that Dave gave to the Ireland team. I'm sure many wondered why Dave was so unceremoniously dumped from the squad. I know I did.

'Dave always gave all he had for Ireland and when he was dropped it crushed him. It turned him into a bit of a recluse. It hurt him so much that he wasn't wanted for Ireland and it had a major impact on his life no question.

'While I didn't see Dave for a number of years due to me suffering from a broken hip, it pained me when I heard how bad Dave's battle with the drink was. I think at that time Dave needed a boost of some kind and he got that boost from alcohol.

'I'm immensely proud of Dave and treasure our friendship. I'm proud of the career that Dave has had and proud that he faced his problems and came through the other side still standing.

'There have been and will be very few players like Dave Langan. He fought for his dream to be a professional footballer and achieved it. The hand of fate didn't touch him on too many occasions, however he remained the same person throughout it all.

'It is great to see him now having gone through what he has. He should be proud of the career he had. He chased the dream and caught it. His service to Ireland and Irish soccer will never be forgotten. His legacy will endure. There is no better way to be remembered.'

Chapter Four

A record signing

Some people make great coaches but not great managers, Brian Clough was a great manager made even better by the fact he was clever enough to have Peter Taylor with him, who was a great coach. Colin Addison was a great coach but not a great manager.

You can get the badges and the qualifications but it is really how you manage people, which make great managers stand out. When I signed for Birmingham I realised that Jim Smith was a great manager. I had only spent minutes with him but immediately trusted and liked him and I knew I was going to join Birmingham after my initial meeting; he did not have to make a big sale to me. Archie Gemmill, and my old friend Colin Todd were both with Birmingham at the time, so at least I thought I would know someone if I went there, which would help me settle in better.

I cannot remember the conversation to be honest, although I do remember him saying to me, 'You're in the Second Division, we are in the First, where do you want to play?'

Maybe that was naive on my part, I did not have an agent and I did not speak to anyone before I went to him, but that said I trusted my instincts on his character rather than the financial side of it.

I think I was right, one of the things I learned about Smith was that he knew how to get the best out of people, he really brought me out of my shell, despite knowing I was shy, Smith was never afraid to have a go at me and he was the first manager I ever spoke back to.

I remember during a training session when he felt that I had not given my all he turned to everyone and said 'look at Langy he just jogged back'.

It was designed to get a reaction from me and it did as I lost my temper and shouted back at him, nothing too bad, just that I had been giving it as much as everyone.

I later apologised to him and he just said forget about it, he was nice man and I enjoyed working under him. We used to call him Mr Angry though, he set high standards for us and if we failed to reach them he was not afraid to give us a lash of his tongue; although he did try and help us learn from them too. He was great on the field and loved to play attacking football, which for me was great.

Moving to Birmingham was a good move at the time and gave me the confidence I needed to kick on. I was named Man of the Match in my first game for Birmingham. I remember we beat Coventry, one of the clubs that had reportedly been interested in me, 3–1 to get our and my season off to the perfect start.

Around the time I first arrived at Birmingham Jim also went out and bought my International colleague Don Givens from Bournemouth but sadly Don did not hang around too long in the Midlands before he moved onto Sheffield United.

It was a good bunch at Birmingham at that time, obviously Colin Todd was there when I arrived and I knew Don from the Irish scene despite his short stint there, but I got to know the lads in the squad very well, the likes of Mark Dennis, Alan Curbishley, Keith Berchin and Frank Worthington were great guys to be around and we were good friends on and off the pitch.

Frank in particular was a smashing guy, not to mention Elvis mad, I got on great with him and we had many a good session together. Frank had a reputation as a bad boy but he actually was not really how people made him out, to me he was a lovely bloke. He was a great player and actually a good trainer, although maybe that's being too kind, as he mainly loved to concentrate on his shooting during training.

He would hit shot after shot and I can tell you he never missed. He was a genius on the ball and he had a lovely touch. Jim knew how to manage him and get the best out of him. He would often leave him alone to get on with things, especially if he knew that Frank was under the influence after a night out.

A lot of the time we came into training struggling from a night on the tiles, we would try and get through best we could and then after training skip on home to bed for a few hours' sleep. It was a good crew though and we all had each other's back. I was one of the quieter ones in the group, that was until I got a drink in me. Drink gave me confidence, the more I drank the more confident it seemed that I got. I would not say boo to you when I was sober but when I had a drink in me you could not shut me up; it also made me more comfortable chatting to women.

I settled well into life in Birmingham, on the field anyway. Off the field things were only going okay, Mandy had remained in Derby and I was trekking back and forth to see her and Elliot, it was not ideal at the time but I did not mind doing it. I missed Elliot and it was amazing how much he had changed every time I saw him. A footballer's life is like a lot of industries; you go where the jobs and opportunities are. I was no different; I didn't want to play Division Two football with Derby, they needed the money anyway so I had to move to better myself and to help my family.

Despite travelling up and down to Derby when I could, I still managed to go out and get to know the players. It was a good squad at Birmingham, with plenty of big names and characters there. There were one or two lads that I got on with extremely well. One of them was the left-back at the time who was a lad by the name of Mark Dennis. Like me Dennis was an attacking full-back and he was very good, playing for the England Under-21 team.

Mark was a lovely fella, and he would give you his very last penny although like us all, he was fond of a drink. I remember one night when I was out with him, future Everton star Pat Van Den Hauwe and Alan Curbishley; it was after a particularly bad result. We had played West Ham away and gone down 5–0, I had been ruled out through illness and instead of taking my place on the bench, I spent the evening in the director's box with none other than the great Sir Bobby Robson.

I had a great chat with him that night and really enjoyed his company. After the game, the lads were heading out and even though I was not well I decided to join them, not the wisest of moves. We headed to a wine bar to get over the loss.

The lads were all depressed and in bad form so perhaps a drink was not the best idea. I remember it was my round and I went up to the bar to get a round of drinks and had just ordered when I heard some noise behind me, some guy just started having a go at Mark, I think he was slagging him off and Mark just reacted and smacked him. The guy was knocked off his feet and we ended up having to leave the bar, I think we were even barred. Thankfully it never got back to Birmingham though or made the papers for that matter.

It was a silly thing to do but these things happen, because we were always out people thought they knew you and could say what they wanted to you. I am sure if it happened today there would be a massive blow out from it but it was different then, footballers were just that, footballers not celebrities.

I got know Mark and Alan very well, I actually lived with Alan for a while when I split with Mandy. Alan was a nice lad, we got on well. I always knew he was going to be a manager, when he was not playing midweek, he would go and watch games. He was definitely a student of the game, even in those days. When we went out, I would be stupid and getting drunk, while Alan was sensible. He married a lovely girl Carol, they were a very nice couple and I am glad he has done well. He was a great player too, a lovely passer of the ball and he formed a nice partnership with Kevin Dillon in the middle of the park for us.

Much like my time at Derby, home form was the key to us staying up and we only lost five games all season at St Andrew's. Typically though, what in my view was a great achievement for a newly promoted side to get to mid table, our 'success' was overshadowed by Aston Villa, who won the title that season.

That said I only played under Jim for 18 months before the club rather harshly sacked him. Smith had got the club into the First Division and managed to keep them there; my first season there. We started the season well beating local rivals Coventry 3–1 on the opening day of the season before we drew with Manchester United and Liverpool at home as well, We finished mid table, 13th, in what was then a 22 team League, so it was a great result for us.

Having secured our status in our first season, our signings for that dreaded second season became that bit more high profile, whereas myself and Don had arrived the summer before, this time around there was an European feel to the team as two Dutch wingers, Toine van Mierlo, who had won three caps for Dutch side in 1980 and Bud Brocken, who would go on to win a couple of caps, both joined us.

Both of them were flying machines, they arrived from FC Twente and I suppose they were a sign of our intent for the new season, sadly they did not make the desired impact and I think after one season both of them headed back to Holland. Sometimes when you bring in a foreign player it works and then other times, for reasons that are purely down to factors other than football, it does not. I think that is why a lot of English clubs went for Irish players in those days, it was close, we spoke the language, could actually play ball with the best of them and usually cost little or nothing. Most the players I knew went to England at the ages of 14, 15 or 16 so there would have been nothing paid for them.

Of course not all the Irish boys who came over made it, I was one of the lucky ones and even with England being so close to Ireland, lads, myself included, got very homesick.

Van Mierlo, I remember had played against us when Ireland famously beat Holland 2–1, he actually set up the Dutch goal that night, although I am sure Gerry Peyton would dispute that. Van Mierlo had crossed in the ball and Peyton, who was a great keeper and reliable as anything, made a rare gaffe when he dropped the ball and the Dutch scored from it. Thankfully we bounced back to win though, as I don't think I would have spoken to Toine if they had.

It must have been hard for those Dutch lads to come over, they did not really know the language and had to integrate themselves into what a predominately English based changing room with some very interesting characters. I often wonder what they would have thought of us.

Sadly for Jim, the board over-reacted to our run of results and he was sacked and replaced by Ron Saunders all in the space of a weekend.

Saunders was the man who had led Aston Villa to their first title in over 70 years and soon enough he was to become my boss at Birmingham. His appointment happened so fast, it confused us all, there really did not appear to be anything wrong with Jim, we had not hit the heights of the previous season but there did not appear to be any problems. We were struggling all right but I think we would have been okay if we had stuck with Jim and I know he would have gotten us out of it.

Saunders on the other hand had fallen out with Villa, I think it was over his contract and he promptly resigned. The Birmingham board reacted almost immediately and sacked Jim and appointed Ron.

Ron Saunders was a tough man. He was as hard as nails. When he came to Birmingham many people thought at the time he was the type of manager that we needed. There were people at the club who began to see Birmingham as their meal ticket. Saunders was brought in to put a stop to that.

His success at Aston Villa guaranteed him a measure of respect when he arrived. Right from the beginning he had me pegged. He would say to me, 'Your positional play isn't good.' Having heard that from John Giles I knew that Saunders was not too far off.

He was fanatical on fitness. When he arrived he would regularly send us on 90 minute running session without a football in sight. It was a shock to my system and I would think to everyone else's.

There were few times that he missed things. After a defeat to Aston Villa he told me that the following week against Southampton he would be counting the number of tackles that I made in the game, so no pressure there then.

When he arrived he told me that he tried to sign me on more than one occasion when I was unhappy at Derby County but Derby refused to sell me, so he must have thought I was a decent player.

He had this belief that if an attacker got by a defender just once then the defender had lost the battle. It was that mentality I suppose that helped him bring the League title to Aston Villa for the first time in decades.

There was not much socialising with Ron. He was not the type of manager that would have a beer and enjoy that side of the game. In many ways it was the way things should have been.

My relationship with Ron Saunders was terrible, we never saw eye to eye at all. One time he even banned me from talking to the press. He had told me not to travel over to Ireland for a game as I had a hamstring injury, I felt fine and reported for duty with Ireland who made their own assessment of whether I was fit or not. Ron went mad when he discovered I had made my way over and fined me two weeks' wages.

He was not happy, as I had told a paper I felt fine and had played the previous weekend without any trouble. I then put in a transfer request as I wanted out, I loved Birmingham and enjoyed my football under Jim Smith but to me Ron was ruining the club. Of course he rejected my request and actually placed a £1 million price tag on my head. In hindsight, given that I had put in a request and therefore had forgone my entitlement to a cut of the transfer fee, maybe it was a good thing that no one came in for me. But I was determined to leave at that time.

I could never understand how Ron managed to hang on to his job at Birmingham, he must have been on a big contract or maybe the board were afraid to get rid of him because of the manner in which they had appointed him; either way, as I said they should never have gotten rid of Jim. The morale at the club under Ron was poor, I remember we lost 4–0 to Norwich and it all kicked off afterwards in the dressing room. At the time we were bottom of the table and really struggling.

Alan Curbishley was raging over the result and the manner in which we played and he accused some players of not trying, which is probably one of the worst things you can tell a player after a defeat. That got everyone riled up and it turned into a big melee, thankfully nothing too serious but we were all fed up with the way the team was playing. These things often spill over whether it is on the training ground or in the changing rooms, emotions are running deep especially after a loss and something gets said and next thing lads have each other by the throat. It is not ideal but at least it shows that people care.

Despite my relationship with the new man in charge, one of my finest moments in a Blues jersey actually came under Saunders would you believe. It was the last game of the 1981–82 season and we were away to local rivals Coventry, we needed a win to stay up. Mick Harford got the winner and I recall the late Ian Handysides playing out of his skin. Ian was a great young player but struggled to hold a regular spot, he left the same summer I did, and I think he went to Walsall although Birmingham later re-signed him.

That match was one of his best games for us and everyone thought he was going to push on and become a great player for us, sadly it never happened for him. He died tragically in the end, a brain tumour I think, I was very sad to hear that. You hate hearing that players you played with passed away, but it is even worse when they are so young. Ian was just coming into his prime as a player and a man, he was so young, only 27 when he passed away.

For me that game is one of his legacies, we all wanted the win so bad. It did not matter that a lot of us did not like Ron or his style; this was not about him, this was about keeping Birmingham in the top division. It was a match of high emotion I remember being absolutely wrecked after it. We won 1–0 and managed to stay up.

We had a great side at Birmingham but a real lack of consistency cost us. We had great ability in the side but we would so often win two games and then lose the next one, the change in the style of football from Jim to Ron made us more predictable to teams.

Ron was a different manager from Jim, whereas Jim wanted us to play attractive football Ron was more interested in getting the ball forward as far as possible. He just wanted us to play the long ball, it was not pretty, I remember his favourite saying was put some snow on it. As far as I was concerned his football was boring and soul destroying.

The lads all hated it, as for me, I had learned under the very best, Brian Clough, as well as Jim and they both wanted us to play attractive football that meant passing the ball forward, it was lovely to watch and great for the fans. I remember as an apprentice under Clough that if you gave the ball away during training you were forced to go and sweep the stands. I loved playing that way and while I considered myself a good defender, I definitely enjoyed getting forward as much as I could. This long ball game was not for me and it was definitely the worst time I ever had as a player on the pitch. There was nothing exciting about it and I did not enjoy going out onto the pitch under Ron.

Ron was a big name at the time though, especially for what he had done at Aston Villa, the best way to describe him was that he was a no nonsense man, there was no banter with him, there were no beers with him after a game and for me there was no style to his football.

At Villa he had a good team with some really good players with the likes of Denis Mortimer, Gary Shaw, Tony Morley and Peter Withe but he did not use them to the best of their capabilities. Although that said it is hard to argue with a man who delivers a first title to a club in over 70 years. The board definitely panicked when they saw he had become available, I suppose as well it would have gone down well to a point with the fans, here they were bringing in a manager who had won the title with their deadly rivals.

Birmingham City and Aston Villa fans hated each other as most city rivals do; it's the same in Merseyside with Liverpool and Everton, the same in Manchester with City and United, London with Spurs, Chelsea and Arsenal and the same as in Scotland with Celtic and Rangers. The Derby game may not be as high profile as these games but try and tell that to the fans in the stands and the players on the pitch. I had never experienced a derby experience like it and if you ever wanted a night to stay in off the beer, go out and lose a derby game to Aston Villa.

Whenever we lost a derby match, you would not be seen out for dust, you kept quiet about it and hoped it was soon forgotten. One defeat that sticks out in my mind is during my first season at Birmingham when we lost 3–0 away to them in front of 43,000 fans. I hated losing at the best of times, but that was hard. I was living with Alan Curbishley at the time and there was not a chance in hell we were leaving the house that night. In my first two seasons with Birmingham I never played on a winning side against Villa, in fact the season we managed to get one over on them I was on the sidelines.

Jim's departure happened so fast in the end though that he never got to say goodbye to the lads. The second year, as it generally always is for newly promoted sides, was tougher than the first and results were not going the way they should have been. We were having a rough ride all right, but I firmly believed that we would have been okay. The board did not think so though, they panicked and sacked him. We had drawn two a piece with West Ham at the weekend, and Jim was gone by the Monday with Ron coming in. I guess they thought that Ron would deliver them the title but in my mind we would have been better off with Jim Smith.

Despite Jim not getting his chance to say goodbye to the lads, I knew he was very upset about leaving and he had every right to be, he had taken the club up and kept them there. More importantly he had done it playing good football. I reckon Jim gave me more bollockings than any other manager I ever came across but he never held it against you nor did I with him. I actually respected him. Jim was a player's manager and despite giving it out to you, he was not called Mr Angry for nothing, he would not have a problem forgetting about it later and buying you a pint.

After he left I took the time to call him at home and tell him that I was sorry he was gone, I remember even still calling him boss. I think he appreciated the call and I remember him saying to me, 'Thanks Langy I will keep you in my thoughts'.

Little did I know then but I would be back playing under him a few years later when he signed me on a free transfer for Oxford. I think it shows how good a manager he was though with the success he achieved with Oxford. That said it would be a couple of years before I would join him at Oxford so I had to concentrate on my club at the time, which was still Birmingham.

Things were different after Jim left though, the football and the atmosphere changed in my opinion. I did not have the same relationship with Ron as I had with Jim and I can tell you that after I left Birmingham I never again spoke to Ron Saunders. I never played in the first team during my last 18 months at the club. I did manage three reserve games before I left but I was never near the first team. Towards the end of my time with Birmingham I remember Saunders told me that I was no good as a footballer and that I should call it a day. I could not afford to quit the game, as there was no insurance cover on me at Blues so I accepted a free transfer to Oxford. I remember when I left Birmingham for Oxford he told me I was finished as a player and would not do well.

That hurt me and there really was no need for it, but I got my own back in the end and took great satisfaction in dedicating my success in the media to Ron Saunders. I remember when I went back to St Andrew's in an Oxford shirt and the home fans gave me a great reception. I was delighted, they were great fans and they, like me, appreciated people who gave their all. The Birmingham lads were also brilliant and I remember shaking hands with them all and them telling me how good it was to see me back playing. I was also delighted by the fact that the greeting the fans gave me would have pissed Ron off no end. We saw each other but didn't acknowledge each other, I think the feelings we had towards each othr was definitely mutual. The atmosphere around the club was not the same after Jim left and loads of players, not just me, fell out with him. Those that did, were usually shown the door, it was his way or the highway.

Mick Harford

Mick Harford was a burly competitive striker at Birmingham who thrived not just on the crosses of Dave but also on the Monday morning banter.

'When I signed for Birmingham from Bristol City they were a big club with some big names and at the time they were in Division One (Premier League). Ron Saunders was their manager and he was one of the reasons I went there, I had worked with him before and had enjoyed it. Dave mightn't agree with me on this but I thought Ron was a good manager and a hard task manager but he had built a good team and it was only when I got there that I realised just how good the team was, key to that was Dave Langan.

Langy was one of the best players at the club and he was ideal for me as a centre-forward being a very attacking right-back. He was more like a winger than a defender in his play. He would get right down the line and between himself and Mark Dennis there was a constant supply of quality balls into the box.

Off the field, there was a good social scene and Langy was one of the main lads in it. He was a quiet man but had a great sense of humour; he would sit there and take everything in, he was very observant and then he would slag everyone off.

I suppose looking back a lot of people demanded a lot of time from him especially in and around Birmingham, but it was a very sociable time at the club, although there was nothing too mad about it. I couldn't wait for a Monday morning, I used to love sitting down with Langy, Mark and Alan Curbishley and having a good chat about the previous weekend.

It was great catching up with Dave last year at his benefit game, I hadn't seen him in years but I think it is a testament to him as a person and a player that so many former players turned up for the game, in fact I can't recall seeing so many ex-players turn up.

I was delighted for Dave though, he deserved it, it was hard seeing him on crutches and the obvious pain he was in but then he'd smile and you'd forget the struggles he had. Dave had a very warming smile, not to mention a great memory, I mean I hadn't see him in 20 years and the first thing is he says to me is 'Can't do no more', which was a reference to Dr Polyzoides, I think that was his name.

At the time I was in pain and no one knew what was wrong with me, I had a hernia, and I was one of the first players to have one. I would go into the doctor and he would tell me "I can't do no more for you Mick", I was so frustrated. I remember meeting Langy one time after coming out and he said to me, "What's up Mick", and I said "Ah I don't fucking know". In the end the doctor had to open me up to find out the problem and thankfully they fixed it, and here I am over 20 years later and Langy can still remember the doctor's name, unbelievable'

Chapter Five

Pulling on that Green Jersey, a dream comes true

Growing up in Ringsend, Lansdowne Road was a throw of a rope away from me and I used to go to all the games there. I was even a ball boy in 1973 when a Shamrock Rovers XI played against Brazil. I will never forget it, Johnny Wilkes had to convince me to do it because as usual I was scared and nervous. It was really an Ireland XI with players from the North and South taking part but because of the problems up North at the time it was billed as a Shamrock Rovers XI. Not that I knew too much about that at the time, I remember walking out with Derek Dougan and Johnny Giles, little did I know then but five years later he would hand me my first cap. It was a wonderful game too, that side, be it an Irish XI or a Rovers XI, managed what no other team had done for 35 years and that was to score three goals against the Brazilians.

It was an unbelievable feat, especially as none of the team had really played together and it was a mixed side. I remember my hero at the time Pat Jennings saving a penalty although sadly Brazil eventually won 4–3, still it was a credible result and really helped put Irish players on the map.

It's funny but while my Dad's team was Shelbourne, I used to support Shamrock Rovers. Dad used to head over to watch Shelbourne whenever he could, while me and Paddy Murtagh would head to Milltown to watch Rovers.

They had a great team in those days with the likes of Mick Leech and Frank O'Neill who were great players and also played for the Irish team. Liam Tuohy was a great manager and they played lovely football. Tuohy deserved his chance at the highest level and eventually got it when he was made the Irish manager and I think he deserved it and sadly while results improved slightly under him, ultimately the job took its toll. It was not the most glamorous job in football in those days and the money on offer was not enough to support a man with a young family.

Tuohy's eventual replacement was Johnny Giles, who was at the time and still is an Irish legend. Giles had achieved it all in England with Leeds United and was highly respected in the game. Although it would be another few years before I came to his attention. It was 1978 when I made my Ireland debut under Giles, the game was at Lansdowne Road against Turkey and it is a moment that ranks as the proudest moment of my footballing life.

Before I made my actual debut for Ireland, I was in contention for the friendly with another eastern European side Bulgaria. However, a poor performance cost me dearly, I had been called in by Giles for another game between the Irish based players and the English based players.

I had gotten very nervous before the game and turned in a shocking performance. Not one of my passes that night found a player and I was given a torrid time by Bohemian's winger Gerry Ryan, who would later join me over at Derby.

I was at Derby at the time and had just turned 21. Johnny had heard about me and he called me and invited me up to play in a testimonial for the Leeds player Paul Madeley. He told me afterwards that there was a big game in a few days and although I would not be involved in that, I would be involved in the next friendly.

True to his word I was called in the squad for the Turkey match, I had grown up near Lansdowne Road so knew what it was like to be at a game, although when I was growing up Ireland mainly played their home games at Dalymount Park.

I remember the game so well, the day before the game Johnny came up to me and told me that I would be playing tomorrow, he said to me 'Don't worry, if you can play Division One football you can play international football'.

I remember walking out onto the pitch before the game, my legs had turned to jelly, then when I heard the National Anthem for the first time on the pitch in the green shirt of Ireland I thought I had died and gone heaven.

I had settled into the squad well beforehand which helped me, Don Givens is someone that sticks out as being very nice, although so were all the players in fairness. I was pleased with how my debut went, we had won 4–2 and I had played well setting up two goals for Ray Treacy.

After the game Ray told me he was delighted with the service he had gotten and told me that I had hit some great balls in. That was great to hear and really good for my confidence. Johnny was also pleased although he did say to me that he would like to see me play against some better opposition to see how I would do, which was fair enough.

After the Turkey game I played in the 0–0 draw with Norway, who weren't the force they were in the 1990s and I had a poor game to be honest, with Johnny taking me off at half-time. After the game Johnny just said, 'I'll talk to you tomorrow'.

He was obviously disappointed with how I had played and while I knew I had played poorly even I did not think it would be another two years before I would pull on the green shirt of Ireland again. He left me out of the squad for the game with Holland and that was how it was for the next two years.

Despite only playing two games under Johnny Giles I did feature in a lot of squads but never made it back into the team. I had not taken my chance against Norway and did not deserve my place especially with West Bromwich Albion's Paddy Mulligan playing so well at right-back for the team.

Although I was not always rosy about my failure to play in the starting XI for Ireland, it was frustrating too especially the times when I was playing good football and not getting into the team, not even on to the bench.

I remember about five months after my debut Ireland was due to play an historic game against Northern Ireland, the first time the two teams had played against each other as separate footballing nations. Paddy Mulligan was injured for the game and instead of Giles giving me another shot to play at right-back, he moved Tony Grealish, who was a midfielder with Leyton Orient, back to play there.

My club manager at the time, Tommy Doherty was livid and spoke out about it. Tommy knew I was a player that needed confidence and I remember him saying at the time, that he was worried, 'that this could knock me back'. Thankfully Giles did not get involved in a war of words with Tommy he was very diplomatic at the time and simply said he had the 'greatest regard' for me.

Although that said I did not even make the bench for the game so I can understand Tommy's stance though, he knew I really wanted to play for my country and after being released from the club for the game not to even make the bench must have been annoying for him.

Afterwards I was depressed, especially as Johnny did not speak to me at all about his decision, I had not played well against Norway and I had not started the season well so I did not expect to displace Mulligan but I still did not expect to be left out of the team and even left off the substitute's bench.

I remember at the time doubting I would ever get into the Irish team at all and contemplated turning down the next invitation I received from the FAI for a game although at the back of my head I knew I would not turn it down. There were players from outside the first division getting picked ahead of me although I think Johnny thought I was too nervous and did not have enough confidence to play for Ireland at the time.

I don't think there was anything sinister in my not getting picked. I think a lot of it was down to my own problems and as I said a real lack of confidence and no matter was what said to me I could not shake it. I was playing in the First Division though and was playing well at times. I wanted nothing more than to play for Ireland and to do well and that might have weighed on my mind a bit.

I think if I had got a run of games though I would have established myself in the side and would have grown into it, as I showed under Eoin Hand but maybe Johnny was afraid to take the chance on me preferring the experience of Mulligan.

Johnny was a great manager though, he was the kind of manager that pulled you to the side and had a quiet word with you, and if you were not in the team he would pull you aside and tell you why. If you made a mistake he would talk you through it so you understood what you had done wrong. It was good management; he treated you like an adult.

His style was a million miles away from Jack Charlton's style; I remember being named Man of the Match against Scotland then missing out on the next squad without any explanation. Giles was a man manager, Charlton was not.

I could never get my head around the fact though that despite being a player manager and concentrating on his own game on the pitch, Giles managed to see everything that was going on around him. He never missed a trick, and he was not afraid to tell players if they played badly but at the same time he was not slow when it came to handing out the praise.

Like Eoin Hand after him, Johnny was unlucky during his time with Ireland and if were not for posts and games we drew that we really should have won Johnny and Ireland would have made it to a major tournament.

I know that Giles did a lot of work behind the scenes to make things better for the players; he wanted it to be more professional. I suppose Johnny would have been used to the best of facilities at the time with Leeds and wanted to bring that into the Irish set up.

He changed the hotels and training facilities; he also was the first to reduce the number of FAI officials to travel to games, it was ridiculous at times, the whole front of the plane would be filled with loads of hangers on while we would be in the economy class, not that this was an issue, I think the issue was that they did nothing to get us there while we did.

There were some nice officials however, Joe Delaney, the father of John, was a lovely man and he was very obliging. He definitely had the player's side. If you went to see him about a problem he would try and look after you and for the younger players in the side who were often short a few quid, he would help you out with a few bob.

I think in the end Johnny got fed up of the pressures that came with the job, he had done a great job and had lifted the profile of the team to another level but I think he took them as far as he could. I don't say this because I could not get in to the side at the time.

I had repeatedly, during his time in charge denied that there was ever a problem between us despite me not being in the side and that is still the case to this day. Johnny gave me my chance to play international football and I will always be grateful to him for that.

Even when he left he had a small role in my third cap, as despite the popular Alan Kelly senior, who had been Johnny's assistant, taking over the side for the friendly game with Switzerland in April 1980, it was really Johnny that named the team and he included me at right-back so it was a good vote of confidence by him.

My game had improved a lot though by that stage and I felt I was ready to stake a claim for a regular place in the line up. Derby County were managed by Colin Addison by then and he had bought in John Newman as his assistant manager. Newman was a good coach and he helped tighten up the defensive side of my game.

He didn't curb my attacking instincts he just got me to also concentrate on the defensive duties, he helped make me a more complete full-back although I was by no means the finished article, I was still improving and getting better with each game I played.

That day against Switzerland was the perfect chance to stake a claim for the right-back spot, I was determined to do well and while I think I played okay that day, the fact that we won 2–0 put a good gloss on things.

I suppose as a defender it was good to keep a clean sheet and that was the main thing.

The players had been behind the appointment of Alan Kelly to the role, he was very popular within the set up at the time and he was a lovely man. Despite Alan winning that day however it was the only game he ever took charge of. I think he had other commitments so he could not stay on in the role, Eoin Hand was his assistant that day and in the end he got the role as the manager.

My best time in an Irish shirt came under Eoin. He was a great manager in my eyes and he was definitely very good to me in my career. My sisters were delighted when he was appointed as he was a real footballing man, and he rated me as one of the best right-backs in England. That backing was fantastic and really helped my confidence. To think that the Ireland manager thought so highly of me was a major boost for me and it helped my game no end.

The majority of my caps came under Hand and he obviously saw something in me that Giles had not, as he trusted me; no more so than when he asked me to man mark Diego Maradona in what was his first game in charge.

Being asked to mark Maradona was one of the biggest honours of my life. Maradona was on his way to becoming the best player in the world at that time and six years later would almost single-handedly win the World Cup for Argentina.

At the time he was still playing in Argentina and despite being only twenty you already knew he was going to become one of the greatest players of all time. In fact everyone knew about him, which was rare in those days, as you didn't have things like the Internet to spread the word.

As always before any game I was nervous as all hell but given that I was going to be marking Maradona I was even more so and I remember a couple of nights before the game I went to the dogs with Gerry Daly and this fella came up to us and said 'how are you going to deal with Maradona?' Daly just turned around to the guy and said, 'don't look at me, Langy will'.

That game against Argentina will live long with me, I can still remember that the grass had not been cut and was still long which was not really suited to a passing game but that did not stop Maradona. That said I was determined to make sure he did not have the easiest of days. My first tackle of the day on him I clattered into him, two minutes later

I got booked for another tackle on him and he just looked at me, but the look said, 'is that all you've got?'

Playing against Maradona was hard as not only were you supposed to mark him but you were also in awe of his touch and skill and it was often hard to focus on watching him. His balance was amazing and he was the best player I ever played against.

Sadly I missed out on getting his jersey after the game as Don Given had made an arrangement with Alberto Tarantini, the former Birmingham defender to get Maradona's jersey although I did get to shake his hand after the game.

That was my fourth game for Ireland and just 11 international games later, life as I had known was about to change. In between I had now become a regular right-back for Ireland and with Hand making his mark on team very quickly we started the 1982 World Cup campaign full of hope.

With players like Liam Brady, who was playing in Serie A with Juventus at the time, my old friend Frank Stapleton who had just become a £1 million player, Chris Hughton, Mick Martin, David O'Leary, Kevin Moran not to mention the emergence of a young Ronnie Whelan, hopes in the country were quite rightly high and we expected to be in the mix to qualify for our first major tournament.

Unlike nowadays where there are a couple of small nations thrown in the mix, back then you were up against the very best straight away so we were paired with France, Holland, Belgium and Cyprus.

It was a tough group but we started well with a 3–2 win over Cyprus, Giles was still in charge for that game so I was not included in the team, however something happened after that game that would reignite my international career; Giles resigned.

After being recalled for the Swiss game under Kelly and starting Hand's first game in charge, I went on to play a big part in the campaign, and played in five of the eight games. We started the group well though and I remember we beat Holland 2–1 at home in our second game.

That was a huge result for us, Holland had finished as runners up at the previous two World Cups and despite going through a transitional period they were still favourites to win the group and qualify.

Eoin though had done his homework and made the right moves before the game when he decided on an attacking formation, moving Mark Lawrenson in to the middle of the park with Liam Brady playing in the hole behind Don Givens and Frank up front.

It was a brave move for a young manager especially managing his first competitive game for Ireland, and it worked. Brady was immense on the night, one of the best games I ever remember him playing. He controlled the game and attacked them at every chance.

I got a lot of praise for my performance that night too, Chris Hughton and myself were the full-backs and we tried to get forward as well as we could without abandoning our defensive duties.

The next game we played Belgium, again at home, this time we could not repeat the form we showed against Holland but there were a lot of positives to take from it. Again I think I had a solid game that day and felt I was really growing into the Irish shirt and what it represented.

After three games in the group, we were unbeaten and had five points, however our next opponents were France, in Paris. It was always going to be a tough game but the build up to the game was marred by some back and forth between the FAI and the clubs in England.

Some of the English clubs were refusing to release our players for the game against France, which was due to take place on a Tuesday, of all days. The night of the game, Birmingham City were due to play Ipswich and Jim had refused to release me and Don for the game. I was livid, I even remember offering to forgo my pay so I could go but he was having none of it.

Thankfully UEFA intervened and ruled that the clubs had to release the players, they also ensured that such a scenario would never happen again as contracts involving internationals would include clauses allowing them to travel for games.

It was a ridiculous rule but it shows just how much power the clubs had at the time and that was just over 30 years ago. Even though you still see the same club versus country rows at every club. It's understandable on their part, they pay your wages and all that, but for me and I am sure every other player out there, the feeling you get when you pull on your international jersey is hard to surpass.

In the end despite a heroic performance we lost 2–0 and the good work began to unravel, for the second time in four years a referee's decision had cost us dearly against France. Back in 1976 a Giles managed team had a perfectly good goal disallowed on their way to a 2–0 defeat and here we were suffering a similar faith.

We were one nil down when Michael Robinson scored what looked like a legitimate goal, however, it was disallowed, the referee indicating that Kevin Moran had handled the ball in the build up. It was a ridiculous decision and cost us dearly.

Eoin was making the right noises though, a large contingent of Irish fans, close to 1,500 I think, had made their way across for the game, it was disappointing that we lost, it was just another chapter in the hard luck story that was Irish football.

After the debacle against France, for which was I was forced to miss the League clash with Ipswich, there was no such trouble the following February when we played Wales. In fact I was released without any hassle whatsoever although looking back now I am not sure I should have gone. We played atrociously that day, and lost 3–1. It was my third loss in an Irish jersey but to me it had hurt more than the defeats to France and Argentina. On both those days we came off the pitch feeling that we had given it a good shot but that day in Tolka Park we were shocking.

We bounced back from the disappointment of those defeats to France and Wales by beating Cyprus 6-0 at home, which was at the time our biggest ever win in an international match, and as we headed into the closing stages of the group, were in contention for the World Cup in Spain.

We then had three big games, two away, to Belgium and Holland and then a home match with France. The away games would ultimately decide our chances of qualifying.

The most controversial of which was the 1–0 loss to Belgium thanks to a late goal and we then drew with Holland 2–2.

For me the game with Holland when we went and drew 2–2 was the one that slipped away, I know a lot of people speak about the Belgium game but if we had won that night we would have been in a better shout of getting there; but hindsight is no sight.

That said I will never forget that night in Belgium when we were robbed, the referee was Raul Fernandes Nazaré. I have, and still believe this, never had a problem losing in football, I might have been disappointed with my own or the team performances but in general there were never sour grapes, except for that night.

I remember the squad had arrived over in Belgium a few days before Eoin and we were all in good spirits relaxing at the hotel and having a few beers, nothing major, as we knew we had a big game. The FAI officials were there as were some of the press, it was all very relaxed; they had an unofficial player of the year award which I won (Gerry Daly was named worst player!! it was all in jest though). The night of the game itself while we did not have a lot of shots on target, we certainly were not the worst side and deserved a point, which would have taken us to Spain.

I remember Frank's goal, there was definitely nothing wrong with it, and it should have stood, but it was not even that decision. Jan Cuelemans who scored the winner for Belgium with just two minutes to go was all over our man for the goal and it was a clear foul. I think that defeat was one of the hardest I ever had to take as a footballer, and it was a low moment. That night we all had a drink in the hotel, I remember Eoin, who was down in the dumps after the game and had a few angry words with Nazaré, tried to rally us all with a version of the rare auld times but it would have taken more than that to get us back up after that.

In between the Belgian and Dutch game we played a couple of friendlies beating Czechslovakia 3–1 at home before losing 3–0 twice in a matter of days to the German B side and the Polish team.

I don't think people read too much into the results however, it was May and a long and successful season for Ireland was coming to an end. The improvements on the field were there to witness and it was time to enjoy the summer before we returned for the Dutch game.

That game in Rotterdam was a tough night for us and I think we showed great character in the way we played. It's a kind of forgotten game for a lot of people but to head to Holland and come away with a point was a magnificent achievement.

Twice we came back from a goal down, Michael Robinson, who was making a real name for himself in an Irish shirt, got the first goal and then big Frank equalised with 19 minutes but we failed to find a winner. To give you a measure of that result in Rotterdam, the Dutch beat Belgium 3–0 there a few weeks later.

I had an unenviable task that night as I was set to mark Johnny Rep, who was probably one of the best wingers that I had ever faced. He was also one of the players that gave me one of my worst nights in an Ireland jersey.

We travelled to Rotterdam to play Holland in a World Cup qualifier and I was picked at right full, meaning that I had the job of marking Rep for the 90 minutes. While it was nip and tuck between us for most of the game there was one moment midway through the second half that I have never forgotten.

Rep had managed to work his way into the Ireland box and I was the last line of defence. Rep rounded me as I put in my challenge. He went down and when I looked around, to my horror, the ref had awarded a penalty to Holland.

My heart sunk and if the ground could have swallowed me I would have been a happy man. I was sick. Admittedly I saw penalties been given for lesser challenges but that did not make any difference at the time.

Looking back it was probably frustration that made me slide into Rep. He was a class player and I wanted to make an impact against him. I made an impact but not the one I had intended.

Frank Stapleton helped me out by getting the equaliser, which saved us from a 2–1 defeat. After the game I was down in the dumps and I remember Alan Mullery, Mike Bailey and Alan Durban all chatting to me and trying to pick me up.

They all told me that I was not the first full-back to be given a hard time by Rep. While that gave me some comfort, I still knew that there were three full-backs in contention for the right full jersey. I was praying that I would hold onto that jersey as we had France at home in our next qualifier.

The group was very tight in the end with just two points between Belgium at the top and Holland in fourth spot, we ended the group in third spot, level on points with France who had a better goal difference.

The trips to Belgium and Holland might have ended our hopes of going to Spain but for me it was the final group game, which effectively ended my career. The game was my 15th in a green shirt and it was against France. While I had been worried that my performance against Holland and Rep might have cost me my place I need not have as I was named in the starting XI.

I came in to the game in good form and had the weekend before just broken my Birmingham goal duck, and it was a memorable effort too. Despite being an attack-minded full-back I did not have too many goals to my name when I made the switch to Birmingham. Indeed I only had one goal to my name at that stage of my career.

The memory of that match is still crystal clear. West Ham United were the visitors to St Andrew's and it was one of those games that you dreamed of playing in as a child. The atmosphere was cracking before kick-off and the intensity off the pitch was matched by the pace of the match. It started off at a 100 per cent and got quicker.

Midway through the game we had an attack down the left-hand side and I was quite forward, looking for the ball. Eventually the ball came to me on my left foot. Now my left foot was generally for standing on, so I did not expect what happened next.

The ball took off and rattled the back of the West Ham net to everyone's surprise, none more so than myself. I suppose if you are going to score your first goal for a new club then it might as well be a memorable one, and that certainly was one that I have not forgotten.

I travelled over to Dublin in high spirits for the France game although this side was certainly a different proposition from West Ham United. Not many people outside the squad gave us much of a chance of getting a result against the French and on paper it was hard to argue with them. That French side contained the likes of Platini, Bellone from Monaco and Girard from Bordeaux.

The feeling within our squad was that we had what it took to beat a team like France, especially at home. There was a real depth of quality in our squad at the time. We were blessed to have the likes of Liam Brady, Ronnie Whelan and Frank Stapleton to mention a few.

One of the biggest reasons we beat France was that we stayed patient. They showed that when we played them in Paris that one of their biggest strengths was passing and moving. They had the players and the skill to rip any team open. If we could stop that at source we knew we had a big chance of causing an upset.

The crowd that night also played a huge part in our win. As is typical of any Ireland crowd the support we got was fantastic. Every supporter that night played his or her part in making Lansdowne Road into a fortress.

What was most satisfying was that we had the self-belief that we could knock over France. Even when we went behind we kept our discipline, shape and most importantly our confidence in each other and ourselves.

That night Ronnie Whelan was playing in front of me and despite being only 21 he put in a fantastic performance, one of the most mature displays for a young player I have seen in a long time.

We took the lead early on, a couple of minutes in, I remember I got to the ball in front of Platini to break up a French attack and the ball ended up on the right wing with Michael Robinson. Frank swept his cross home and the ground erupted, it was a fantastic start and a great goal.

The tackle that ultimately ended my career came in this game. Looking back there was not too much in it, it was not a vicious tackle but even now I can still hear and see it in my mind. I think it was a fella by the name of Alain Couriol, although a few tackles flew in around that time, there was another lad Larios who also went in afterwards too.

The tackle came into the side of my knee but it never entered my head to come off, not that it would have mattered, I remember John Devine telling me I was not coming off anyway. My knee was killing me but even now when I see the videos of it, you would never think anything had happened, but I was in severe pain.

It was a fantastic game though to have played in, we never let them settle, we took our goals well and deserved to win. At one stage we were 3–1 up although they bombarded us in the final 20 minutes, and Platini scored with a nice finish. I remember near the end of the game thinking I might have given away a penalty.

The French had a player on the wing called Didier Six who was a very good player and he gave me a tricky afternoon. Towards the end of the game I thought I had fouled him and was relieved when the referee waved it away. I would have hated to have been the man that had cost us a famous win.

The group was very tight in the end with just two points between Belgium at the top and Holland in fourth spot, we ended the group in third spot, level on points with France who had a better goal difference.

We will always look back on that Belgian game though as the night a World Cup appearance in Spain was cruelly taken from us. But we had done Eoin, the fans and ourselves proud with our displays in qualifying, no one could have doubted the commitment of the team and the brand of football was different to anything the fans would have seen before; like Johnny Giles, Eoin Hand was an extremely organised manager and knew how he wanted the game to be played.

He took things on another step too as he wanted to ensure that the team always had the best of everything although it was not always possible with the resources we had available. But he certainly tried.

From a personal point of view when I look back at that campaign it was a roller coaster journey, not many teams beat Holland and France and still fail to make a major tournament. Looking back to the French match in particular, I suppose I was an idiot, I should have come off sooner.

The atmosphere was amazing that night and I was so pumped up in the game, I felt better than I ever did. The adrenaline was just pouring out of me. It was only afterwards the pain started hitting home.

Even now I don't think I would have done anything differently and while I am in pain these days, the pain I was in that night had little effect on me, it did not stop me having a few pints and enjoying the craic that night back in the Green Isle hotel.

I can understand why managers in England hated us all, English, Welsh and Scottish players included, going on International duty. There was often some great session with lots of drinking especially after a famous win. That night was one of those nights and it was a hell of a party.

The Wolfe Tones and Paddy Reilly came down for a singsong with us and so did the Furey Brothers. I had become friends with them at the time, as I loved my folk music. It was a great singsong although it has to be said that not all of the players would have a drink, they still enjoyed the craic they just would not get drunk. My old best man Frank Stapleton never used to have a drink.

The injury I suffered in that French match kept me out of International football for almost four years. I missed the 1984 European qualifying campaign where again we missed out in a tough group with Holland and Spain, finishing third.

I made my international comeback on the 1 May 1985 when I was called back in to the squad for the World Cup qualifier against Norway. Again we were put in a tough group and faced the USSR, Denmark, Switzerland and Norway.

When I was injured Eoin Hand was one of the few people that kept in touch with me, he used to wish me the best of luck and told me he had not forgotten about me, which was great for my confidence.

It was no different to the treatment I received at Birmingham, nobody really wanted to know about me, I remember Mick Harford, Mark Dennis and one or two others called in to visit me in the hospital but after that I heard from no one, not even a phone call.

That is the way it is though, you are a waste of time to everyone, you cannot play and you are not at training so you are out of the loop and not part of the banter, not really part of the team. It can be hard for any player to be forgotten about like that and I was no different.

That's why it was good of Eoin to keep in contact, it made me feel that even though I was not able to play, even though I was not even in attendance at the games, I was still an important member of the Irish squad.

I did not even come home during the years I was injured, a small trip aside, so I did not see my family unless they came over to visit me.

When I eventually got back fit, he was true to his word and rang me to tell me he was delighted to have me back and he had included me in the squad for the game against Norway.

That he would include me in such a game was a great boost for me and when he told me I was starting, it was like making my debut all over again. I was so excited; here I was finally getting to pull on the green jersey of Ireland again. It was like a new beginning for me, a second debut.

The players were fantastic too, I remember big Frank and Kevin Moran coming over and giving me a hug, they made me feel so welcome like I had never been away.

I was named in the starting line up and got a great reception of the crowd, which was great. I managed to play the full 90 minutes, however, sadly the game itself was a bit of a non event and it finished 0–0.

We were brutal and did not play well at all. Irish fans are a good set of fans in general, they will appreciate a bad result if they see you giving 100 per cent and I felt I had done ok if not anything ground breaking, however I don't think they were too happy that day. Neither were some of the players and I remember Liam Brady who had played no worse or no better than anyone on the field was taken off.

Liam was not too happy about being taken off and was quite rightly upset about the way we had played, he ended up having some small words with Eoin, nothing major, but I do remember him saying that things were not working out.

The pressure was mounting on Hand ahead of the '86 campaign and there were rumours that he would not stay on when it was over. When you look back at his reign, the games with Belgium and France in Paris will always stick in the mind.

Eoin just needed a little luck to make something special happen. When you see the luck that Jack or Giovanni Trapattoni had, you can only imagine what Eoin would have done with it.

It was a fantastic team and deserved to play on a bigger stage then they did, although thankfully some of them got the stage they deserved when they played in Euro '88 and Italia '90.

Eoin was a great manager though and like the players, deserved to manage on a bigger stage. He was a great man manager and from what I could see he was very close to the players, I know he was good for my international career and he definitely helped me in my footballing development.

He defended you to the core and always had the player's back, especially in public, which is what you want from a manager. Nobody wants their dirty linen aired in public and if you had a bad game, you already knew it without it being made even more public by a manager slamming you.

Not only was Eoin a great manager, he was also a great singer and when we had team nights out he loved to get involved in the banter, and loved the craic and especially loved a good singsong, he did a lovely version of the rare auld times, which was his song. I'm a big fan of the folk songs too and loved a good singsong in those days.

My love of music stems from when I was a youngster growing up in Ringsend in Dublin. Actually from my teenage years, music and film have both played an important part in my life, in and out football.

When I played football both in England and with Ireland, I loved a singsong after the match and I would always sing Irish Folk songs. I was a big fan of the Furey brothers; I got to know them quite well during the 80s and often had a good drinking session with them. I first came across them when my friend, Paddy Murtagh, whom I had my first taste of gambling with, asked me to head up to Wexford Street to see a band called the Furey's.

I had never heard of them at the time, but I remember Paddy telling me 'sure we'll head up anyway and have a bit of craic'.

I loved them, I thought they were brilliant that night, I didn't have any of their songs but really enjoyed them and it grew from there. I used to always buy their records, tapes and CDs and one time I even took some of the Oxford squad to see them when they were playing locally. It was a great night, about eight or nine of us headed along to see them. We had a great evening with them, a few beers and a singsong, the lads loved it.

When I was stirring my memory for the book, I looked through my old scrap books and I came across an interview I had done for Shoot magazine. It was a gas to see my answers, all of them would have stood up today, the likes of, 'If you didn't play football what would you do?' To which I replied, 'I'd be on the dole' which was true and others about my biggest influence, which was and still is John Wilkes.

One of the answers I gave though was not true and to this day I don't know why I said it. The question was 'Who is your favourite musician?' I said 'Elton John'.

Now I have nothing against Elton John, in fact I do quite like *Candle in the Wind*, however, I had at that time never listened to or bought an Elton

John album. It was funny to read it, I must have thought no one would have known the Furey's.

One of the other things I was asked was what was my favourite film and that answer is of course, as my family can testify, *Shane*. When I was a kid my dad told me that the film was on down at the Carlton on O'Connell Street and I should try and see it.

I went along and I remember the first time I saw it, I hated it. I told him I had loved it, but I did not enjoy it all so I went back and watched it a second time, I don't know why, it was important to him I suppose, so I wanted to give it another go.

The second time I saw it I loved it, and have seen it easily about 300 or 400 times since, my sisters call me Shane all the time and Audrey tells me that she thinks the reason I like it is because in a way I can relate to Shane, played by Alan Ladd.

When I got fed up with things I used to move and I never settled, which I supposed used to be true. I have a great picture that they got for me of Alan Ladd and we have it sitting proudly at the top of the stairs. It would not be everyone's cup of tea but I love it.

I often used to put *Shane* and another great film *The Quiet Man*, with John Wayne, on when at Oxford and we were travelling to away games on the buses. The lads loved it, especially Billy Whitehurst. He went and bought it himself I remember, he used to watch it loads and would then come and practice his newly acquired Irish accent on us.

Movies were a great way to keep out of the pub too and a couple of times a week after training I would head to the cinema to catch a film.

Since I have left football, I still watch movies and enjoy reading, I especially love autobiographies. I love reading about the Hollywood actors, Steve McQueen, Humphrey Bogart and John Wayne not to mention the footballers. I loved Paul McGrath's book, it was so honest and refreshing especially from a footballer who experienced the transitions from the recession days of the 1980s, when I played, right up to the early days of the hype of the Premier League.

There is a great story of Paul and me that has never seen the light of day, until now that is. We were out in Dublin after an Irish game, I cannot recall for the life of me which one, I would not mind but I was sober for that part of the day.

We ended up in Rumours night club on O'Connell Street which would have been really popular back then, we were drunk heading there, and it turned out to be a bad move as we got ever drunker in there. We eventually left there about 3am and stumbling on to O'Connell Street we came across some people who were pushing a wheelchair up the path.

We ended up talking to them and as a prank we took over and began pushing the wheelchair about. Everyone was in great form, people were taking pictures of us and we were signing autographs all round. The fun came to an abrupt end though when the local Garda came along, saw who we were and promptly dropped us back to our hotels. That was one way to get a taxi ride home in Dublin. It was great craic though and harmless fun.

Paul was a great guy though, one of the nicest fellas you could meet, I remember when his autobiography came out, he actually sent me over a signed copy, I could not get over how brutally honest he was throughout the book. It was a real eye opener and while I admired what he had done I could also relate to a lot of what he had written.

I also read Ronnie Whelan's book, which again was another good read from another fine footballer. But just one small point that needs clarification – In his book, *Walk On*, Ronnie speaks about being dropped by Jack Charlton for the game against Brazil and his place given to me.

Ronnie goes on to say that Jack told him he was going to start on the bench and play me left-back. Ronnie to his credit was a very versatile player and a good one at that, he was part of that great Liverpool team of the 1980s and perhaps in my mind, he should have been utilised in the middle for Ireland on more occasions. But such was competition for places it was difficult to accommodate him there.

Anyway Jack's plan all along was to have the option to spring Ronnie from the bench and to mix it up a little if required.

Now maybe the whole thing was a conversation that took place and nothing more but the thing is this, I actually did not start the match against Brazil and I certainly did not play left-back. My left foot was for standing on, nothing more! I came on as a substitute in that game with 30 minutes to go and at the time we were 1–0 up thanks to that great goal by Liam Brady. Thankfully we held on to achieve a fabulous result.

As I said it is not a big deal but I just wanted to have my records straight, although I am sure there will be words in black and white here that people will also dispute, but that is how people recollect sometimes, I suppose memories can get a bit distorted over time.

I remember after the game that Jack gave out to me for showboating;

me, showboating against the Brazilians. I don't think so; I never understood that one, although I don't think I ever understood Jack.

Ronnie to his credit was a nice fella, and I got on well with him. Like me he loved the old Irish folk songs and was not afraid to belt them out. He was a great player and I don't think anyone will ever forget his goal against the USSR in 1988, what an unbelievable volley definitely the best goal I have ever seen scored by an Irish player.

Heading away to Ireland matches, especially the home ones was a great experience and one I used to love. I loved heading down to see my Ma, I loved being back in Dublin and I also loved the buzz of knowing you were going to pull on the green jersey of Ireland. For me that was what being a footballer was all about, playing for Ireland. I think if Ireland had been a club team I would have been very happy indeed.

I roomed with a few different players when I was with Ireland. I used to room with Ray Houghton a bit, as we were pals from Oxford. I also roomed with Paul McGrath as well as Jim Beglin.

I remember Conleth Meehan, a friend who helped me get my benefit dinner from the FAI, telling me he had met Jim one day and they briefly got to chat and the subject of me came up.

Jim told Con that it was me that got him into the drink and I have to say that this sadly is the truth. Jim was a nice fella and a good defender, he could have been one of the all time great Irish defenders but like me, injury played a cruel part in his career, although I am delighted to see that he has now carved out a successful media career.

When Jim came into the Ireland set up first, as he was a full-back I used to room with him, that was the way it was then and I imagine it still might be that way, you often roomed with the players you would be playing alongside so you got to know each other a bit and developed an understanding of each other. It was a good idea, although with the many different personalities in football I imagine it doesn't always work.

Thankfully I had no such experiences with any players and actually I got to know Jim very well in those days. After a game in those days I, along with the rest of the squad would hit the pub for some drinks and a singsong.

Despite being a shy character, once there was drink in me I was the opposite and I used to love a good singsong. I knew a lot of the songs too and would have no problem after a few beers belting out the old Irish songs.

As I was sharing with Jim it was only natural that he would come along with the boys and me and join us. I could not tell you how much or how little he drank though, I am not even sure how much I drank. I remember though when he broke his leg, it was an awful thing to happen, especially as he was such a promising player. I did write to him to wish him a speedy recovery and again through no fault but my own we have lost contact over time.

Niall Quinn

Like so many of the younger members of the Euro 1988 squad Niall Quinn had grown up watching Dave Langan running up and down the right-hand touchline for Ireland and later on he experienced first hand just what playing for Ireland meant to Ringsend's favourite son.

'The earliest memory I have of Dave Langan was when I was a child growing up in Dublin. My parents took me along to Lansdowne Road to watch the Ireland games and one of the standout memories that I have is Dave Langan tearing up and down the wing for the entire 90 minutes of each game that he played.

'He would not stop running for the whole match. He was so keen to be involved in the match and tried at any moment to get involved. I could see even then just how much it meant to him playing for Ireland. The keenness and eagerness to help his side shone through.

'Indeed there was one occasion that I have never forgotten. Ireland was playing at home and I went along as I always did. Dave was playing of course and was flying into challenges and flying down the wing as was heis wont.

'A person standing behind me, I think it was a Dublin man, was watching Dave shoot down the wing and on one occasion that Dave passed us the man summed Dave up as a "Trojan" and to me that sums Dave up perfectly.

'Dave was a Trojan in everything that he did. He had a passion for football that few people had. Be it from having tears in his eyes when the national anthem was being played, to trying to teach the squad members Irish folk songs, Dave had a passion in his heart that could not be quenched.

'Along with his pride the other thing that jumped out at you about Dave was his pride. He had immense pride in what he did and where he came from. Dave took particular pride in wearing the green jersey of Ireland.

'That meant so much to him. He would have bled for that jersey and he made sure that everyone in the squad felt the same. When I came into the squad and got to know Dave you felt that there was an onus on you to represent the Irish jersey to the best of your ability.

'Dave took the pride that came with wearing the Irish jersey to a whole new level and that attitude prevailed throughout the whole squad. Some people nowadays see playing for their country as glamorous. Dave saw it as a huge honour and took that honour and the responsibility that came with it very seriously.

'The honour and responsibility that Dave instilled in all of us certainly rubbed off on me. There were times during my international career when I would be called into a squad for some meaningless tournament at the end of the season and the manager would say that you did not have to travel over if you did not want to.

'But you would think back to Dave and think what would he do? Anytime he was called into the Ireland squad he would be there and that attitude would make you forget about your holiday that you had planned and you would pack your gear and head off to wherever you were playing.

Indeed it was something that I tried to pass on to the younger players whenever they came into the squad. That's why it's good to see the likes of Robbie Keane, Kevin Kilbane and Shay Given still having that passion and desire to play for Ireland whenever they can.

'Off the pitch Dave was exactly the same. That same passion that made him such a success on the pitch was matched off the pitch. You would go a long way to find a nicer guy. He always had a smile on his face and was very down to earth and humble.

'I rarely remember seeing Dave in a bad mood. He was always smiling or whistling and was genuinely great fun to be around. He is still very old school in some respects. If he saw you chewing gum with your mouth open you might get a sharp word in your ear.

'But that was just Dave. Total respect from start to finish and anyone who has met or played with Dave should have the same respect towards him, because as genuine people go Dave was at the top of the League.

'It is a shame to see Dave fell on hard times. But everyone who played with him will never forget the difference that he made to Irish football when he played. A lot of the values he has, courage, pride and passion may be missing slightly in modern football but Davey brought them everywhere he went.

'Although we have not had much contact in the last while I hope Dave knows that the years of service that he gave to Ireland didn't go unnoticed. Every supporter that watched him play knew that he gave his heart and soul for the Ireland team.

'He also gave players an understanding of what it meant to be an Irish soccer player. What it meant to run out in a jam-packed stadium for your country. He had a fire in him that fuelled his footballing dreams and the fire he had sparked off in countless people after him and for that Dave should be very proud of his meaningful contribution to Irish football.'

Chapter Six

18 months of hell

After the injury against France for Ireland back in 1981, I returned to my club and missed the League Cup defeat against Nottingham Forest on the Tuesday, and then the following weekend I was out against Southampton, which I think we won. My left knee was in a bad way and I was in agony. The elation I had felt after the French match was long gone and had been replaced by pure pain. The knee was pretty swollen at this point and I was out of action for a good few weeks, although at this point, there was no mention of an operation.

The club's physiotherapist told me to rest up and I was given cortisone injections to bring the swelling down, there was nothing I could do at that point. I was in and out of the side over the next few months.

There was a lot of fluid in the knee and it never felt right, I was basically playing, putting ice on my knee, resting, getting physio and playing. A lot like Paul McGrath used to do when he had the troubles with his knee, I was not training at all and my fitness was suffering as a result. All I could do was gym work, which meant doing weights, but there was no running, I was just about making it through games. I did not feel free in my knee and I could not play well, I had an awful constant pain in my knee.

I was also getting treatment to the knee, they used to do an ultrasonic on it, which was basically running little currents into my knee. It did not seem to be working though, I was still in agony.

Things had to come to a head and eventually they did in February 1982, we were playing at home, it was only Ron Saunders' second game or so and I took a heavy knock to the same knee. I was in agony and I had to go off, which is ironic as it was the best I had played in a matter of weeks.

The next morning my knee was massive and completely swollen, so I headed into the physiotherapist who told me my knee was gone. He sent me to the specialist, a Dr Polyzoides, who told me he was going to cut a hole in each side of my knee and do an exploratory operation.

Basically he put a camera in and had a look around, they thought I was out and even though I was not fully with it I could still hear what they were saying. The specialist was going on about how the cartilage was badly torn and then he saw the root cause of my problem, I had an ulcer the size of a 50p piece in my knee.

What was initially an investigation into what was wrong was suddenly an operation to remove an ulcer. Each knock I had taken on my knee caused this ulcer to grow and grow. Dr Polyzoides had to drill the ulcer out and then take some marrow from my hip to rebuild the cartilage around the knee.

When I came round from the operation, he was there with me and said to me 'I have some bad news for you, you are going to be out of the game for six months'. I didn't know what to say, I had not been expecting this at all and I certainly was not prepared for it. His words are a blur after that; he said something about the operation being very serious and explained what he had done, but I did not take any of that in, all that was going through my head was that I was not going to be able to play football for the next six months.

He told me that I needed to rest up for three months and not do any jogging or running, I would not been able to anyway so there was nothing I could do. Naturally I was devastated and immediately turned to the drink to help me through it, they put on crutches and I basically spent the next three months hitting the bottle. I don't remember too much of that time, I was living on my own and was in a bad way. It was only the start of things to come.

After three months, I was told to build up the knee slowly by doing a bit of jogging. Even though I was drinking I had not put on much weight and was still in okay shape but that first day of jogging, I knew something was not right, I felt a sharp pain in my knee and went straight into the physio.

He told me it was nothing serious, gave me a cortisone injection and told me to go home, rest up and that we would try again next week. The following week when I went to jog the same thing happened again, it was a sharp shooting pain in my knee, I thought to myself ah jaysus something is not right here, so back into the physio office I went.

This time I was sent back to Polyzoides who said he was going to have a look inside the knee again as it was swelling up. He opened me up and sure enough he found the problem, the new cartilage, which had been built from marrow from my hip while setting well, was breaking off in small pieces called gristle, and these pieces, were catching me causing the shooting pain. I was relieved as at least the problem was not me and I was not imagining it. He removed them and stitched me up. Once again I was told to rest up and wait for the stitches to come out before I started jogging again.

I was really fed up with everything, but knew I had to give it time. I will admit I was impatient at times but it is hard when you are an injured footballer as no one wants anything to do with you. The club don't want you around. They don't even pay you, it is actually the Professional Footballers' Association (PFA) that pays you.

There was to be no third time lucky however, as I started my latest comeback from the knee operation, the first time I went to jog again I immediately felt the same pain I had before. By now I was a regular in the physio's office and I went straight into him and he simply told me to put some ice on it, rest and we will look at it tomorrow. I think at this point they were getting fed up with me and thought that a lot of the problems I was having were in my head.

I went home and rested as I was told, the next morning I woke the knee was still sore when I jogged so it was back to Dr Polyzoides. He actually said to me this time, are you sure you are not imagining this? I said no Doc I am in agony.

I was about to have my third knee operation in a matter of months, he opened my knee again and once more he found loads of pieces of gristle. I could tell he could not understand what was going on. He removed the pieces again and I was told to rest before starting light gym work and to lay off the jogging for a couple of weeks.

I started to do my work in the gym again, there was no point disobeying orders and trying to jog. So I worked solely on my upper body, I was determined to get into good shape. One day I was on the mat doing some stomach exercises when I twisted from left to right, suddenly I was in agony once more, only this time it was not my knee at all, it was coming from my back.

I struggled to get up off the mat but eventually did and went down to the physio once more, it was the same face only with a different story this time, I've done my back in I told him.

I would say he did not know what to make of me at this stage, once again as he done each of the other times I had come in to him, I was told there was nothing wrong with me and to go home, rest and we would look at it in the morning. I knew they all thought that because I was struggling with being injured that it was all in my mind. I stupidly did as I was told and went home, I had one of the worst nights I ever had and could not wait for the morning to come. I had to get a taxi and it was one of the most uncomfortable rides I ever had in my life.

The physio had a look at me and I was on my way back to Dr Polyzoides, I could have made my way to his surgery with my eyes closed at this point.

The doctor said he would take an x-ray of my back, and when he came back he delivered the second knockout blow of my career telling me that I had cracked my vertebra and would need to have a cast put on my back. The idea was that the plaster would ensure that my back did not move and would knit itself back together.

I was forced to wear the cast for about eight weeks at which point he did another x-ray and discovered that the crack was still there. I was now forced to wear a hard back corset, like a woman would wear, with a steel back on it. I kept this on, and I don't know how as it was the most uncomfortable thing ever, for four weeks. When they took it off, they thought it had worked, however the very first kick of a ball in training my back went again completely, the only thing for it now was an operation.

My spine had widened at this point and this was the problem, I was facing another six months out of the game; I was not going to play anymore in 1982, the year was a total write-off. I was now having my fourth operation of the year and I can tell you to this day I have never forgotten the pain I felt when I woke up. As it seemed was always the case these days Dr Polyzoides was there when I woke up and despite the pain I felt, he told me that everything had gone well and that I now had two steel bolts in my back.

I remember asking would they be in there the rest of my life and he said no that I would need another operation to get them out and I just thought, 'Ah jaysus.'

As I lay in the bed, horrendous pain shooting through my body, all that I kept thinking was I am the worst man of steel ever, Superman would be ashamed of me.

There was nothing I could do however this time, I was bandaged up and had been told to go home and rest. I was seeing a girl at the time by the name of Dawn and while I made her life miserable she was kind enough to help me through that period as best she could.

Three months in and I went back for a check up and for once everything seemed to be going right, my back was healing nicely and I was ahead of schedule. My knee still was not right though but he said there was nothing he could do with the knee until the back was healed so there was no point even worrying about it.

The plaster eventually came off the back and I remember feeling like a horse had kicked me, the pain in my back was so bad. My back was all bruised and the blood had clotted a bit so I had lumps there. It was a sight for sore eyes but at last I seemed to be on the mend.

I was wrong. The first time I jogged, the knee still was not right and I could not believe it, I was in a state of despair. I thought this is it I am finished in the game, it just so happened that around that time Birmingham's own club doctor, a fella by the name of Robson, I cannot for the life of me recall his first name, came to visit me.

I must have been in some state when I answered the door to him. I had been drinking heavily the night before and was at my lowest ebb, I was clinically depressed at this point I reckon. I had been through the mill and still was not fixed, it did not seem fair at all and I failed to grasp it all.

Anyway this doctor, Dr Robson, takes one look at me and asks are you ok, you don't look too good? I told him I was fine and he said are you sure you are ok mentally? You're not thinking of doing anything stupid are you?

I was shocked, I knew I was depressed and I knew I had been drinking a lot but it never crossed my mind to do the unthinkable and end it all. He told me I was to call him any time I needed to talk or help and to lay off the drinking that it would not help with the depression. I never did call him.

During all this meanwhile Dr Polyzoides had now decided that I needed another operation, my sixth, to cure the knee. This time he was going to open my knee up completely and see if the problem could be found. He discovered that my kneecap was the cause of the problem and filed it down so it was smooth. I was now facing another six weeks of rest and another six weeks of drinking.

The cycle continued once more, I felt good after the operation and went for a jog, this time the back was sore, into the physio, who tells me go home and rest, back in, right back into the surgeon. If it was not so serious it would have been farcical. I know everyone was trying their best for me but it was so frustrating to be opened up every few weeks and being told now you are brand new only to find out you were not. My seventh operation involved an anaesthetic and a lot of injections into my back to bring down the swelling that was there. When I came round, the good doctor asked me to touch my toes and believe it or not I could. I was over the moon the end was finally in sight. He brought me back down to earth though fairly lively, he still had the bolts to take out, I was going to need one more operation on my back.

I felt great after the latest operation though and my knee was doing good too, but it was short-lived as once more I broke down only this time it was both physical and mental. My knee swelled up again and I was back in the familiar surroundings of the physio's office, I just sat there crying this time, there he was saying my knee's gone again, there was nothing from me, I was cracking up and did not know how much more I could take. I was ready to give up my dream of being a footballer. I had at least had a couple of good years in the game and would be remembered as someone who had shown a lot of promise until injury prematurely ended his career. It was tougher to take in than any operation or pain I had been through in the last few months.

This time I was not told to go home and rest, there was no 'we will take a look at it in the morning', they had seen my breakdown and acted. I was once more taken to Dr Polyzoides and he drained my knee, and gave me some injections. I was told to rest for 48 hours.

At this point my injury and failure to recover was pissing Saunders off big time, he was getting fed up of hearing reports that I had broken down yet again in training and faced another spell out on the sidelines. The team was not doing great while I was out and he was under pressure. The usual questions were being asked of me, was the sore knee just a figment of my imagination? I had been out injured a long time, was my state of mind okay? Was I depressed? The answers were simple, no I was not imagining my injury, I did not want to be injured and feel pain and yes I was depressed. But I was depressed because I knew that something was wrong, every time I tried to jog I still felt a sharp pain. Another operation and yet more gristle removed, I remember Polyzoides telling me he could not keep doing this.

The bolts were removed, it meant another 10 days out. I was used to it by now. I was told it would leave a small scar, I didn't care at this point. Ron called and told me the club would not be renewing my contract and that I would be free to leave. I kind of knew that I would be going, it's hard to justify a new deal when you cannot even run.

I tried jogging again, the same pain returned. I did my usual steps at this point. I remember this time Dr Polyzoides saying to give him one more try. He was a great surgeon and had operated on all the Birmingham lads that needed it. I remember he found what was wrong with Mick Harford when no one else could. I trusted him and believed he could fix me, he decided to open the knee once more and he cleared it out completely. It worked a bit, I could now train but was still in a bit of pain.

I was living with Gordon and Margaret at this time and I was on crutches when one day I got a call from my old boss Jim Smith who was now at Oxford. He said I hear they are letting you go for free and I said they are, boss. Even though he had not managed me in almost two and a half years I still called him boss. How are you, are you fit? I lied and said I was. I remember Gordon was in the background telling me to tell Jim I was on crutches and to be honest. I could not though, I knew that if I said that I would have never signed for Oxford.

I managed to get a few weeks running and I felt good, Jim had told me that he wanted me to come down to Oxford for pre-season training in July. I went back to Polyzoides to have a look at the knee, I told him I was being let go by Birmingham and had a chance with Oxford so he had to get me right.

He decided to have a look at my right knee too as he thought that the pressure on it might be causing some of the problems. For my 11th operation he trimmed the cartilage on my right knee and told me to rest for three weeks.

It was getting near the end of the season now and once again I got a call from Jim, this time asking me if I would be able to come down earlier for pre-season training. I lied and told him there was no need I was doing my running around the pitch here and that everything was grand.

Gordon was on to me now to come clean but once again I could not, I will never go to heaven for the amount of lies I told Jim Smith. I got the stitches out of my right knee and managed to get some lightweight training before I headed down to Oxford.

Smith was delighted as he thought I was in great shape, but in truth I had actually only three days of training before I turned up trying to earn a new deal at Oxford. The Oxford physio gave me the once over and I am sure he knew something was up, I remember him saying that I had very little muscle in my knee and had I had an operation recently? I lied again and said I had had nothing in four months. I am sure he saw through my lie but credit to him he never said any more about it and instead gave me a programme to help build up the muscles in my knee.

Things were now back on track again, I was able to train and play and while I had lost a yard of pace I was doing okay. The knee only gave me trouble once more while I was at Oxford and I had to travel back to Birmingham to see Polyzoides again, this time I was fast tracked through the actual National Health system and not private. I felt bad about this as I was jumping the queue before people who had been waiting ages but I was told not to tell anyone about it. This time I was only out for a week, he cleared the knee of the gristle.

In total 48 pieces of gristle were picked out from my knee, I have kept some pieces and they are at my mother's house in Ringsend, a reminder of the dark times.

A couple of hamstring injuries aside, my body managed to stand the physical strain of competitive football although given the injuries I had suffered and the operations I had endured it was inevitable that they would come back to haunt me and they did.

I was at Peterborough when that happened, and I was playing shit. My back and knee were both giving me trouble now, and I went to see two separate surgeons who both advised me to call it a day and give up the game. I remember the surgeon who looked at my knee saying that I had no cartilage, no ligaments and hardly any cruciate ligament in my left knee. As I did not have any insurance from Peterborough, my injuries meant that I was a real liability, I managed to get an insurance pay out of £2,500 from the PFA with the club agreeing to pay out the final six months of my contract. My life as a footballer was over, a new life was about to begin, what it would entail was anyone's guess.

The pain did not end when the football did however, I remember one time I was forced to wear a neck brace to correct a spinal problem and had to have both legs encased in plaster mouldings for eight weeks. It was a hard time, they discovered a fracture and shin splints, and I was referred to the Park Hospital in Nottingham. Thankfully the PFA picked up the MRI scan costs, which were £750, a hell of a lot of money, especially to me at that time. I was forced off work for six months from the council and in the end the only reason I went back was because if I did not, my pay would have gone down to half pay and I could not afford to be reduced down to that.

One of the worst things about the injuries was the way I suffered when

I went to pick up my children, Callum and Leah. Both were very young when my football career ended and never knew life with a footballer. I remember that nearly every time I went to pick them up, I would get a shot of pain through my back. It used to break my heart and I just wanted to hold them.

The pain in my back was hard to take, and very frustrating. Every time I would get an attack of sciatica in my back, I would take the pain killers but they only worked for a short while and I can remember getting spinal epidurals similar to a pregnant lady in my back to numb the pain. I missed being able to pick up my kids though, at least I could do that with Elliot as I had not suffered the injuries then but it was harder with Leah and Callum.

Two of a Kind – Dave and Big Paul

Paul McGrath is widely regarded as one of the best players to have ever put on the green jersey of Ireland and yet like Dave, Paul, has suffered throughout his life with personal demons. These demons bonded the two men as teammates and roommates.

'From the first time that I met Dave Langan the first thing that struck me was his energy. On the pitch Dave was a ball of energy. He charged around the pitch like he had batteries in him, he just never stopped. He was the most energetic player that I have ever played with.

'Aside from having masses of energy, Dave was also an excellent footballer. Although he was a full-back during his career, I always felt Dave fancied himself as a striker; such was his eagerness to always be involved in the game.

'It was that eagerness and energy that should have meant Dave played at Euro '88. The decision not to bring Dave and a few others to the Championships was a strange choice, and one that I didn't fully understand. I know personally that I would have loved for Dave to be involved and I know the rest of the lads in the squad felt the same.

'It wasn't just the players that felt that way; it was the ordinary fan that wanted Dave there too. The Ireland fans took to Dave because he gave everything he had when he pulled on the Ireland jersey. In every game that Dave played, he left everything he had out on the pitch. He was a selfless player and that fans understood and appreciated that.

'If Dave had made the squad for Euro '88 it would have been the pinnacle of his career. It is a shame that he wasn't given that opportunity, however knowing

Dave he would accept that in life, sometimes you don't get everything you deserve.

'While most people would have known Dave for his on the pitch exploits, I knew other, hidden sides to Dave. You see Dave is a naturally quiet guy. He, much like me, would not rush to be the centre of attention. At the time we would have been young enough and having a drink or two when we were socialising gave us a lift, it helped us settle in and mix with people.

'That lift soon became a crutch to Dave. We both have gone through similar problems and we leaned on drink to help us cope. We were given quite a bit of freedom when we were young guys and there were times when we abused the liberty that we had.

'There were times that I saw Dave very low. Dave would admit that at times he overdid it, yet he was still a fundamentally a good guy at heart who was struggling at the time.

'While Dave was down on his luck for a long time, the night we had the fundraiser in Ballyfermot showed that a lot of people cared about and held Dave in great affection. As an ex-player there is almost a moral duty to help a former teammate.

'I was delighted to help out with the fundraiser. If anyone needed my help or support I would try my hardest to be there. It was the least I could do to help out a friend like Dave.

'I can only speak for myself but I know that the majority of players that played with Dave would have helped him anytime they could. He is one of the most likeable guys that you could meet and when you combine that with his talent, desire and passion on the pitch, you could only like Dave.

'It is mark of respect that so many people have helped him through the years. Everyone that knows Dave wants to see him healthy and happy. We all know that he has had his problems, however the most important thing is that Dave is in a good place and thankfully that appears to be the case.

'Looking back I think that Dave's greatest legacy will be with the fans who continue to remember him and his style of play to this day. I was having lunch with few friends a couple of months ago and when I mentioned Dave's name they instantly recognised his name and the memories of him tearing down the right wing at Lansdowne Road came flooding back.

'To me that is the iconic image I hold of Dave. A guy who was so proud to play for his country and a player who would give every drop of blood and sweat that he had in him to win. He ran his heart out for club and country until he could do it no more.

'Dave wouldn't stop or quit and I think that has helped him overcome the troubles he went through. He has that never give up and refusal to quit attitude that carried over from his professional to his personal life.

'I think that when people mention Dave Langan in years to come he will still be held in great affection by everyone that had the privilege to see him play. That is his greatest legacy to be remembered and held in such esteem by the fans that took him to their hearts and refuse to this day to let him go.'

Chapter Seven

Bouncing back with Oxford

Despite being an attack minded full-back I was never the most prolific goalscorer and throughout my professional career I only scored seven goals.

My most prolific spells were at Birmingham and Oxford and while I only scored three goals during my time there, one of those ranks as one of my greatest moments in football when I scored against Arsenal past my hero, the legendary Pat Jennings. One of the other goals I scored turned out to be much more important, it was the goal that secured Oxford the Division Two title and with it promotion to Division One for the first time in their history.

It was a great feeling to win the title, and even nicer to score the goal that clinched it. It meant that after six years I had my first medal in English football and it meant a lot to me, I was also glad to have won under Jim Smith. Mr Angry, as the players knew him, took a chance on me and I will never forget him for that.

At Oxford I had lost a yard of pace and had to adapt as a defender, despite being only 27 years old. I still loved to charge up and down the field but had to be more careful so that I could get back to do my defensive duties, I enjoyed that season in Division Two and it was a great feeling to not only play attractive attacking football, but to actually play football.

I had almost forgotten the feeling of coming off a pitch knackered from giving it my all, the feeling you got when you won a game and despite my desire to always win I was glad to be back in a situation where I felt something when I lost. For too long I had felt self pity and depression so to be back playing football was fantastic and all down to Jim for taking a chance on me.

It was a shame that he never got to manage us in Division One although QPR were a big draw at the time, so it was a hard decision for him no doubt, I don't think his relationship with Robert Maxwell helped at all.

A picture of innocence – me on my communion day.

Me, Siobhan and Billy.

My father with me, Billy, Siobhan and Audrey.

Celebrating my player of the year trophy with Don O'Riordan.

Derby team photo, that's me beside the gaffer.

Running onto the field of play at the Manor Ground – I loved playing in front of the Oxford fans.

I'm not sure if Siobhan was a bigger fan of me or
Charlie George.

So happy – me and Dawn together.

An old teammate, me with Ray Houghton.

Me with John Wilkes and his family.

Con, me and Niall Quinn.

Con, me and my son Elliot.

Me with John Byrne, who I played with at Cherry Orchard.

With Con and long-time family friend Danny Larkin.

Steve Staunton, me and John Aldridge.

Me and an old friend, Frank Stapleton.

With Frank and my old mentor and friend John Wilkes

How much for this lot? Some of the best Irish players ever to pull on a green Jersey.

Johnny Giles, me and Jimmy Holmes.

My mother surrounded by my sisters, Siobhan and Jacinta with Elliot.

My three children, Leah, Callum and Elliot.

One of the highlights of my career – playing against the great Maradona.

Paul Magee, son of Jimmy, a closed friend who sadly died in 2008.

Two Irish Legends and me – With Paul McGrath and Johnny Giles.

On a club trip with Derby to Benidorm with Don O'Riordan, Colin Boulton, the pub landlord and his wife.

Another signed picture for Siobhan – this time it's Colin Todd.

Who is this moody upstart? Not happy at losing a training game.

I never knew what to make of Maxwell, for one thing he always wore a bow tie, which I never understood and he would always come into the dressing room. To set the scene prior to any arrival of the Chairman into the dressing room be it at half-time or full-time, chances were that Smith would be ff'ing and blinding us out of it, as I said his nickname was Mr Angry and it was for a reason. However, as soon as Maxwell would walk into the room, the atmosphere would change not to mention the language.

Everyone would go quiet, you could almost hear a pin drop in there, eventually Maxwell must have noticed it because one day he turned and said to Smith, 'What's wrong with the boys, Jim?'

Being honest, what was wrong was he should not have been in there, it did not feel right having him there. Maxwell wanted to be the main man and he did not like Smith, and he especially did not like that the supporters liked Smith more than him.

But despite that, it was Maxwell himself who contacted me and told me I would be staying at Oxford.

As I had spent 18 months out of the game prior to joining Oxford I had only been offered a one year deal and when the season finished I actually thought I was going to follow Smith out the door, my contract was up and although I had thought I had done well enough I was not sure how it was going to go.

I need not have worried, as Maxwell rang me at my home and told me I was staying. I was delighted; I had enjoyed my season in Oxford and had really liked the club and especially the fans. Even when you had a bad game they had your back, they never told you that you were useless or anything they were always very positive, 'We'll do it again' is a phrase I remember hearing a lot.

Smith going was a big loss for us, he had created the team and was a great manager. He might have been known as Mr Angry but he got us to gel and I don't think another manager would have done the same with the team at the time. The man who came into replace him was Maurice Evans, we did not know too much about him before he came, but if Jim Smith was to be known as Mr Angry then Evans should have been known as Mr Quiet. He did not say much but was a lovely man and an absolute gentleman.

That first season in the top flight was amazing, the season before we had played teams like Carlisle United, Oldham Athletic, Huddersfield, Grimsby and Shrewsbury although like today it was still very competitive with the likes of Birmingham and Manchester City (without the riches they enjoy today), who both went up alongside us not to mention teams like Leeds United, Blackburn and Wimbledon.

However, now we were among the big boys and for Oxford that was a great achievement suddenly we were playing against the likes of Liverpool, Manchester United, Everton (who were a big club at the time), Chelsea and Arsenal. It was where you wanted to be as a player and as a club.

Of the three clubs that went up that season, ourselves and Manchester City managed to hang on, we finished 18th in the 22 man League while City finished three places ahead of us in 15th. Sadly my old club Birmingham finished second bottom and made a swift return down to Division Two, while we stayed up by the skin of our teeth, beating Arsenal 3–0 at home on the final day of the season.

Personally I found the season hard, the pace was a lot different from Division Two and I struggled until about halfway through the season when I finally got used to it. I knew we had a good team although I was worried we did not have the strength in depth that other sides had at the time.

I have played in a lot of great stadiums during my time in the top divisions but White Hart Lane and Anfield are two of my favourite places to have played at. I used to love when we would have to head down to London to play Spurs, White Hart Lane is a lovely ground, the crowd are really close to the pitch and it makes them really hard to play against. One of the best thing about Spurs is that no matter what, they always play lovely football, back then and today, it does not matter when, the football is always pleasing on the eye. Harry Redknapp, who managed me briefly when he signed me for Bournemouth, is a man who likes to play good football and he did a good job down there.

The other ground close to my heart is Anfield, which is unlike any place you can either visit or play, it is an emotional place, right from your arrival to the sound of *You'll Never Walk Alone* you feel your heartstrings being pulled. I am not sure what it is about the place or how they have created that feeling but it is really unique in football to find a place like it. Of course the home fans are a large part of that, I don't think I have ever come across fairer fans, if you did something good they were good enough to clap and appreciate the footballing side of it. They were always patient with their managers and players and never really got on their back, it was rare if it did happen. Even now, you got the same feeling despite the hardship they went through with the American owners; they always had the managers' and the players' back even when results were not going their way. It is always good for a player to have the backing of his fans, it makes you want to put in that extra bit more, it makes you want to bust a gut to get back to get that tackle in or to the bye-line to get that crucial cross in.

Modern day teams forget about how much of an impact the fans have, as I said it was lovely to play at Spurs where you had the crowd so close to you. I think sometimes clubs are too quick to move ground just to get a bigger and better stadium. You might be able to get more bums on the seat but you often do not get the right sort of bums.

Old Trafford is another fine stadium to have played in, United of course, were not the force they are now when I played against them but again like Liverpool and Arsenal, they always had a sense of history about them that made you think you were beaten before you even got on to the pitch to face them.

The pick of the bunch for me though was the Manor at Oxford United, I loved running up and down the slope and the fans always had your back, just like Anfield in a way.

Our home form and fans was the key that first season in the top flight as I think we won seven games at home and only three away. No matter how we played the fans always had our back and they were the proverbial 12th man in those fantastic couple of years. No matter how we played they backed us 100 per cent and it really helped running out onto the pitch knowing that they had our back. They deserved the Division Two title and Milk Cup success just as much as any of the players.

That first season we started with a draw away to WBA and then drew with Spurs at home. Our best result of the season was probably in our third game as we beat Leicester 5–0, however our unbeaten start ended away to Birmingham who beat us 3–0.

The rest of the season was a struggle although one of the highlights was when we managed to draw with Liverpool 2–2 in front of our own fans although they played us off the pitch that day and we needed a bizarre own goal from Ray Kennedy to rescue a point for us.

It was a great result to draw with the best side in England at the time. I also remember my return to play on the pitch of Old Trafford against Manchester United, before the game I was down in the Stretford End warming up when I heard a voice shout out 'Davey Langy, how you doing?' I looked up and despite the crowds of people there I managed to pick out the face of an old friend from home, Christy Barry. It was funny coming all the way to Manchester to see an old friend. We had a good auld laugh about it the next time I returned to Ireland. The game itself was pretty unforgettable, for us anyway, I am sure Christy Barry went home happy as United thrashed us 4–0.

I did not get to meet him after. Generally after a game there were a few of us that would head into Oxford. While my worst time for drinking was during my time at Birmingham, I was still a social drinker although I never drank to the levels I did when I was injured; the summer of Euro 1988 aside. At Oxford I was back playing regularly and enjoying life again, sure there were times when I let things get on top of me but it did not seem to affect me too much. Playing football was a great way to clear the head, when you are running up and down the right touchline you are so knackered after a game that you don't have time to dwell on life's problems.

At Oxford there was a good bunch with the likes of Bobby McDonald, Mick Moore and Billy Whitehurst who all liked to socialise. We had some very good sessions together and would often start at a lunchtime and finish the next morning.

I remember when the Furey brothers came to Oxford we started at midday and came out of the Penny Farthing pub at 6am the following morning. It was a good time though and while the drinking was still heavy, stupidly I did not worry about it too much as I was with good company.

I said at the start that I like to place a bet and that was true, it was never large amounts though, a £10, £20 or a £50 here, big enough I suppose in those days although one time I went too far.

We used to get tips from some of the lads that worked at the Hern Stable. We had gotten to know them through Trevor Hebbard who lived near one of the lads, I in particular got to know them and used to get calls from them on a regular basis with tips. Generally these were good ones and as I said, while it was big enough money at the time, I was not betting huge amounts.

One time we got a call saying that there was a certainty running at Newbury, the horse's name, it's one I will never forget, was Silk Thread. She was a two-year-old and our contact told us there was no way she would get beaten. Bobby Mc and I, decided to put a large chunk on it, the odds were very good I think she was in around the 6/1. I decided to put on £500, the total of my winnings for the year so far and by far the largest amount I had ever bet on a horse.

We had an away game at Watford that Saturday and travelled down, we were preparing for the game when the result came in, the horse finished second. I had just lost £500. I thought I was going to die, I remember Bobby telling me to get my mind right that we had a game in less than two hours. I was falling apart but somehow managed to get it together. To make matters worse I was marking John Barnes that day.

As it turns out I played so well that they took me in for a drugs test after game, someone watching the game must have been impressed by me and must have wondered where the hell I had gotten all that energy from. I was so mad with myself though for losing that money I never stopped going for the whole 90 minutes.

On the coach back home I said to Bobby, you and me are going getting locked tonight, which we did. It did teach me a valuable lesson though, there are no certainties in life and it is one I remembered, I still bet but smaller amounts, a couple of quid here and there. To be honest, I have never had a lot since I left football, so drinking and football took a backstage while I catered for my family needs.

To this day I still cannot believe what I did that day, I was a right fool.

The highlight of my time with Oxford was getting to the Milk Cup Final. Winning the Division Two titles was a great feeling, being back in the top division of English football was also pretty amazing, however it was nothing compared to winning the League Cup, which ranks as my best moment in English football.

The summer we won promotion Jim Smith had left us and had taken over at QPR, who would only finish five places above us in the table.

It was almost ironic really that we would get to Wembley and face the man who had pretty much put this team together.

We had a nice run to the Final, only playing Newcastle and Aston Villa from Division One, we played Northampton in the first round winning 4–1 over the two legs before we beat Newcastle 3–1 at home, Norwich at home, again 3–1 and Portsmouth at home, yet again by the same three goals to one margin.

I remember the win over Portsmouth as we played in front of a really low crowd, I think only a couple of hundred people turned up as fans spoke with their feet and boycotted the game over the increased costs of tickets.

The 1980s were a hard time for a lot of families and people did not have money at all, oddly enough it is very similar to how things are now. Unemployment was very high, and there were no jobs about so people were being forced to leave the country. I suppose unlike now where people who used to have money are finding now that they do not, back then despite people not having anything a lot of people were used to never having had anything.

I know from growing up in Ringsend what football meant to people, we had very little back then and made do with what we had. For me, even then football was a release, a way of life. I was never happy unless I was either kicking a ball or watching a ball being kicked so when the prices went up, one of the last avenues people had for a break away from the normal way of life was taken away from them.

The crowds came back for the semi-final and saw us pitched against Aston Villa, just five years previously Villa had won the European Cup so they were one of the clubs we aspired to be. The first leg was at Villa Park and finished two goals apiece, John Aldridge scoring both goals.

Aldridge was a fantastic striker; he was unbelievable for us that season and scored over 30 goals. I got to know Jimmy Greaves, as we used to call him, very well as we were also in the Irish squad together. He was a nice fella and a great striker.

I was actually the one who got John Aldridge and Ray Houghton involved in the Irish set up. During my time at Oxford, Ray and John were both in the team and we all got on well, I used to room with Ray in fact. One time after we had played a game for Oxford, we are all sitting in the bar having a post match drink and John turned to me and in his scouse accent told me he was eligible to play for Ireland, next thing I hear a Glaswegian accent pop up telling me the same thing. I told them they must be taking the piss, but they were both adamant and told me that their grandparents were Irish and they would love to play for Ireland.

I told Joe Delaney, the former FAI treasurer and father of John, about Ray and John and he told me he would look into it and follow it up. It wasn't long before they were both called into the team. I remember Ray played his first game against Wales, which was also Jack Charlton's first game, and he travelled over with me. I always used to head down to my Ma's when I came over for games and this time I bought Ray with me and the two of us had a big feed down, Ray was bursting after it.

The Oxford lads loved the fact that a scouser and a Scotsman were in the Irish team and they used to take the piss something terrible, they would come up to me and tell that they had a dog called Paddy, could he play for Ireland? It was all in good fun though and helped build the spirit of the team.

Everyone in the team knew that John was destined for a bigger club and there had been rumours all season that Liverpool would look to bring him back to Merseyside. Being honest no one begrudged him the move, as he was the reason we stayed up. He scored 23 goals that season and finished just behind Ian Rush and Gary Lineker in the top goalscorer charts, two of the great strikers of English football.

I remember sitting on the coach with him when he said he was going up for talks with Liverpool, he was gutted to be leaving Oxford but at the same time he was delighted for the chance to be joining his hometown club.

After drawing the semi-final away, there was a real confidence around the team that we could make our first major Final. The atmosphere around the club was great and the banter too among the players, we all felt we had a real chance of the reaching the Final and the fans played a large part in the second leg. Jeremy Charles and Les Philips scored the goals that gave us a 2–1 win over Villa and a trip to Wembley.

The semi-final win is a bittersweet memory however, I was out of the team at the time so failed to play in either leg. I had injured my hamstring a few weeks earlier and a fella by the name of Neil Slatter, who was a good young player at the time, had come into the team and done a good job. I could not have expected to walk right back into the team but I was still disappointed not to play against Villa. When we won I did not know what to think, I was delighted for the players, they deserved it, but for me, I was down. I thought I had missed the chance to play at Wembley.

It is very hard to be involved when you are not playing; of course you put on a brave face and join in with the boys but if you have not played you feel like you did not contribute to the win. Despite playing in all the other games that got us as far as the semi-final the fact that I did not play against Villa to be honest, felt like I had not contributed.

In the lead up to the Final itself, Slatter hurt his knee in training and sadly for him he would not play any part in the Final. Naturally I was gutted for Neil. He had deserved his place in the team and had put in some good performances, however I was also hopeful that I might get the chance to replace him in the team. Maurice pulled me aside a couple of days before the game and said to me, 'You better be on standby', alluding that I was in contention to start the game.

The Thursday before the Final I went up to Maurice after training and said to him that my three sisters were coming over and I did not want to pay for them to come over and watch me sitting on the bench. I had put him in a corner and I knew it, but I needed to know either way. When I heard him say the words, 'you're playing', I was over the moon, I was finally going to play in a Cup Final in Wembley. I immediately rang my mother and my sisters and told them, they were delighted and I could not wait to see them.

When you look at the programme for the Final you get an idea of just how close I was to not playing as it has all the players bar me in there. If he had been fit, Neil would have definitely started over me.

The day before the game, Maurice had booked us tickets to go see Tottenham Hotspurs and Manchester United at White Hart Lane, the idea was for us to relax as a team and enjoy the build up to the Final. I had agreed to meet my sisters at the ground to give them their tickets for the Final, they were delighted to be over and especially to be going to a Final, it promised to be a great day.

The Final itself will live long in my memory, as I have said it was the highlight of my English football career, although nothing will ever top pulling on the green shirt to play for Ireland. We were up against a QPR side, managed by the man who had taken a chance on me and gotten me back playing football and had already beaten Liverpool, Chelsea, Nottingham Forest and Watford on their way to the Final.

The morning of the Milk Cup I was a nervous wreck, I nearly did not want to play, it was such a massive occasion, I was the type of player that needed to be playing every week to get my fitness and keep it up. I had been in and out of the team and I was not sure how I would feature. I remember bumping into Cloughie before the game and he said to me, 'Enjoy the good times, because the bad ones are around the corner'. That was it though, I had been around enough bad corners to know where they end up and I did not want to go around another one.

Likewise the legendary Steve Perryman, who had just joined the club in March as a player coach, although he was not able to play as he was Cup tied, told us all the morning of the game to enjoy and take it all in. I wish I had listened to those words because even though I have a video of the game and have watched it on many an occasion I cannot remember too much of the actual game itself.

Before the game, it was very tense. The manager Maurice Evans did not really say anything to us, what could he say, we knew what we had to do, I think his only words to us were, 'Does everyone know what they have to do?' We all knew, we had to stick to our game. We had to stick to our passing and moving game and keep it simple.

However, I was terrified and worried about how it was going to go. My legs felt heavy and I thought my hamstring would snap before I even got onto the pitch. Walking out to the pitch took a lifetime and even then my legs felt heavy and then the game started.

After that it is nearly a blur, I know now that I could have run all day for you and felt as fit as a fiddle. Football did that to me, it made me forget my worries and fears and that day, out there on the Wembley grass I felt like I was at my fittest. The supporters were fantastic that day, they cheered us on and if ever there was a 12th man on the pitch it was that day.

My old friend Trevor Hebberd opened the scoring just after half-time and when Ray Houghton scored I knew it was going to be our day. Jeremy Charles sealed an amazing 3–0 win for us and we were now among the big boys.

I thought it was a lovely gesture at the medal ceremony when Evans, who Steve McClaren quite rightly called a gentlemen, because he was one, pushed Ken Fish up to take the medal that he should have gotten.

Fish had served Oxford as a trainer for more than 20 years and had given so much to the club, so it was a lovely thing to do.

Malcolm Shotton was the captain and he was the first up to get the trophy. Malcolm was a great defender and alongside Gary Briggs formed a strong backline. He had come to the club from non-League football and had played with the club in the Third Division so he knew life before we reached the big time, so it was fitting that he got to lift the trophy.

I finally got my hands on it when it was passed down and it was amazing to hold it, I had one side and Ray had the other side. It was a brilliant feeling.

I remember going over to Slatter after the game and offering my medal, even though I wanted that medal more than anything in the world I knew Neil had played his part in getting us there and did not deserve to miss out. He would not take it though and just said to me, 'Ah Langy it's fine'. I had to make the offer although I am not sure what I would have would have done had he said 'Thank you' and taken it.

Afterwards in the dressing room it was mayhem, we had champagne and everyone was singing, I remember I sang The Mountains of Mourne. We were all messing about, spraying champagne everywhere, when in walked my old manager Jim Smith.

It is a measure of the man that Smith, who no doubt would have been feeling pretty low, came into the Oxford dressing room afterwards to congratulate us all on the win, he even shook hands with us.

The bus journey home was pretty special too as all the way up the M1 Oxford fans would beep us every time they passed us by. It was a great night and I will never forget it. We all had dinner together and got pretty locked before making our way to our homes.

The next day I got a call from Jack Charlton to make my way over to Dublin for the game against Uruguay which was only two days later. That did not bother me though, I was ready for it. I actually missed out on the open top bus tour around Oxford with the Milk Cup to go play that friendly against Uruguay. That did not matter to me though; my country had come calling for me.

Ahead of the Final, the Oxford edition of the Cup Final book had a two page spread on the team and I remember at the time all the nicknames we had within the squad. It was a very tight knit team and we all got on, I suppose that was the key to our 'success' during those couple of years.

I was known as Langy, however we had some fantastic names for each other, I remember Trevor Hebberd was called Nijinsky, Jeremy Charles was known as Gorgeous Gus, my old roommate Ray Houghton was Sweaty, Alan Judge was the Flying Pig, Gary Briggs was Rambo; he was a tough lad, Bobby Mac was Jock while Les Philips was called Bellies after Bells Whisky. One of the funniest of them all was Maurice Evans who was called Hello, Hello.

There was great camaraderie with the team though and they were not just teammates they were all friends. I lost contact with them all over time but whenever I did meet up with them it was always like we had just spoken the day before.

Trevor Hebberd

Trevor Hebberd was a member of that Milk Cup winning team and remembers Dave fondly.

'You had to really know Dave to appreciate him. He was a tremendous character and a unique individual. When Jim Smith first brought him to Oxford, I did not know he had suffered so much with injury and had spent a bit of time out of the game, you would never have known it as he just slotted straight into the team like he had always been there. He was a great fella and a gentleman, he loved his football but sadly he also loved his horses and his drink.

'There was a fella who lived near me, Alan, he was a stable lad and used to get on so well with Dave. Alan would give Dave all sorts of tips but a lot of them were bad tips. That same chap eventually got a job about four or five miles up the road with the Queen's horse trainer so the tips became more frequent for Dave, this time these were a bit better, in that he won some. Dave and Alan would always be on the phone to each other.

'I caught up with him recently and he did tell me that he still enjoyed a small bet on the horses, now though it's only a couple of quid, but back when he was at Oxford he was putting 10 and 20 quid on a horse; while not a fortune was decent money at the time considering we did not earn the money that the players today do.

'When Dave came to Oxford there were a lot of characters in the team, some good and some bad, it was that era really, you had to have characters in your team and Dave was certainly a unique character. At first he seemed shy but when you got to know him you realised that wasn't the case at all.

'He certainly fitted in well in the changing room and he had a nickname for everyone. I remember I was known as Nijinsky. It was a great time to be at Oxford though, we won two promotions and the Milk Cup; for a lot of us, probably Dave included it was the best times of our careers.

'The game was probably a bit more physical back then compared to nowadays and I remember Dave was a good trainer although he always looked like he was knackered! In those days we all played with our socks down, there were no shin guards or anything but it never bothered us, we never worried about things like that. Everyone enjoyed it under Jim Smith and Maurice Evans, there was a good bond within the team and Dave was certainly part of that.

'But he was also a very good full-back and if you look at that Oxford team, John Aldridge and Billy Hamilton scored a lot of goals for us but when you look at them you will see that most of them were probably created by the right boot of Davey Langan.

'The last time I met him, after the benefit game, I actually thought he looked really well. He seemed to have found peace with himself. I met his wife Dawn and she seems to have had a good effect on Dave and despite the pain he is in, he seemed really happy which was good to see, he had a tough time of it though so he deserves this.'

Take two, Jim Smith

Not many managers get the chance to sign players they rate highly; even rarer is the chance to sign these players twice but that was what Jim Smith did when he signed Dave, firstly for a record transfer fee back in 1980 then on a free transfer just four years later.

'The first time that I heard about Dave Langan was in 1980 when I was at Birmingham City where I was manager at the time. We had just been promoted to Division One and were on the lookout for an enthusiastic and talented full-back to help take our team forward. I sent my scouting team with the brief to find me such a player and they came back with Dave.

'In fact Dave's name was the only one my scouting team came back to me with. All the reports that I read about Dave were glowing, they spoke of how he was such a committed, fearless and determined player on the pitch and the scouts recommended that we sign him as soon as possible.

'We did what we had to do and we signed him for what was a club record transfer fee at the time of £350,000. When Dave arrived at the club the first thing you noticed about him was what a genuine guy he was. Dave was always in good form and most of the time you would hear him whistling before you would see him coming. He had an infectious personality and became a favourite within the dressing room almost immediately.

'Indeed he became such a favourite in the dressing room that he gave everyone in there at the time nicknames. He christened me "Mr Angry" which was rather funny and probably somewhat true at the time. But that was Dave, always wanting to enjoy himself and be able to have a laugh and a joke with people. He was very much a people person.

'When he was out on the pitch Dave parked the nice guy attitude he had off the pitch and he became this unbelievably competitive player who wanted to win at any cost. He was a bit of a bully on the pitch.

'He wanted to win so badly all the time. He was good for the team in that respect as he drove the team on when things weren't going so well. Dave would always be chirping away and encouraging lads to keep their heads up and keep going.

'Not only did he have a fantastic attitude on the pitch but he had the skill set to go with it. As a full-back Dave had it all. He was a quality crosser of the ball, he had pace and was very attack minded. He was a player that always wanted to be involved and loved bombing down the wing.

'The only thing that Dave lacked was his height. He was a shade on the small side but that never held him back, in fact it only made him more determined that he wouldn't be pushed around on the pitch. It hardened him even more and he became a rock for us during his time with us.

'He never stopped giving everything that he had and that was the one thing that I remember about Dave. His character and attitude he showed on the pitch was a 120 per cent all the time. Few players have that but Dave was one.

'I remember one story about Dave that typifies the man he is. I had moved on from Birmingham and I was managing Oxford. I heard about Dave and how he had fallen on bad times with injuries and everything else and I invited him down to train and play with the Oxfords reserves.

'Despite the injuries that Dave suffered from he still had a lot of ability and was due to play a reserve match one Friday evening quite late into pre-season. Paul Lynch was our first choice full-back at the time and he was down to play the following day for the first team.

'On the Friday however, Paul was injured and there was no way that he would be fit for the following day so I asked Dave, who was only working his way back to full fitness at the time, would it be possible if he could play the Friday and the Saturday as well?

'Dave looked at me and I knew my answer straight away. Dave would play. Not only did he play in both games but he was outstanding in each game. That said a lot to me about the type of player Dave was. Anything that was asked of him he would do. He put his body on the line for the team and that is an attitude that you cannot buy.

'I saw Dave a few months ago and I was delighted to see that he was in fine form. He stopped down to Oxford and asked me if I would be part of the testimonial that was being put together. I jumped at the chance to be involved and was proud that Dave asked me to be a part of it.

'We chatted for a long time about the old days and memories that we shared together. He was in good spirits that day and it was great to talk to him. Dave was and still is one of the most genuine people that I have met in the game. He was always good for any team that he played in.

'It is a shame that injuries deprived him of some of his career but he can be proud of the lasting mark that he made on the game. He was a great player and above all is a great person.'

Chapter Eight

Jack and me – the end of my career

Not being selected for Euro 1988 ranks as one of the major disappointments in my life, it broke my heart not to make the squad and I never fully recovered from it, even now it still hurts me to think about it.

I could never understand how I failed to make the squad, I had featured throughout the qualifying campaign and I played the two games of the group against Luxembourg. I really should have been on the plane over to Germany, I know that Chris Morris was emerging at the time and he was a very fast defender, much faster than me, but I think with my experience I still had a lot to offer and I would have been a useful player to bring, plus I was a better crosser of the ball than Morris.

Ireland's football under Jack was very direct and with John Aldridge as a target man up front, the balls needed to be accurate and that was something I could have provided. I knew John from my Oxford days and knew his game. I am not saying that if I had travelled Ireland would have won the European Championship but I think that given the part that I had played in getting us there and the experience I had, that I felt I should have travelled over to Germany.

What made it worse was that Jack did not even call me. He was not man enough to ring me and explain why after playing throughout the qualifying I was suddenly being cast out in the cold. I know how he felt and he said that if a player was injured and in his plans then he would call him. I had no idea that I was not in his plans, playing in half the qualifiers, including the final game to me constituted being in someone's plans. It made no sense to me.

Even now it still hurts although I am not as angry about it now as I was back then. I think what makes it worse was when I did meet up with him, he told me he did not have my number and that was why he never told me. For me it was a disappointing way to be treated by someone who was and still is a hero to the Irish people, I just wish he could have been more honest and open with me.

It was an incident that Jack Charlton felt obliged to write about in his own autobiography and until now I have never had the opportunity to tell my side of the story and clear my name. I think it sums up my relationship with him. That Jack felt obliged to mention what happened in his book and for me to respond even though it's 15 years later; it's about burying the past and telling my side of events.

In his book Jack wrote that he thought I had been an excellent full-back, which was good to hear although it made my exclusion harder. He also said that he had not seen me for months before he bumped into me at a friendly game with Poland before they headed off to the Euro's. (At the time I had not been named in the European Championship squad and it was well documented that I wouldn't be travelling to Germany.)

Jack said I had clearly had a few drinks and was giving him a bit of lip. I can tell you that nothing is further from the truth, I was not drunk that day and I was not one bit aggressive with Jack even though and many will agree I did deserve some form of explanation for being dropped.

However, being who I am, I left it and did not confront him; I did not even have any interest in going to the game only Joe Corcoran had persuaded me to go. A friend of mine, Sean Farrell, whom I had known since my school days had a couple of tickets so we all went along.

Sean had a few drinks before the game but I did not have one drink before the match, anyway up we went to the game and no sooner am I in there I meet John Byrne. John asked me, 'did I want a drink?' I said, 'grand', no sooner have I the pint in front of me and barely a sup taken, when I have a tap on the shoulder, it is none other than Jack.

As you would expect with so many people around Jack is all smiles and he shakes my hand and asks how I am doing. It was all pleasantries. Then he tells me he did not have my phone number hence the lack of an explanation for my exclusion from the squad. I say, 'That's fine no problem, let's just leave it'. He then said to me 'do you want to come down and train with the squad for three to four days?' and I said no problem. He even went as far to add that I could come and stay with the team in the hotel, hardly the actions of a man that had just been abused. I then said, 'I hope ye do well', which was true, more than anything I wanted Ireland to do well at a major tournament, my own anguish aside I was still a supporter and proud of the national team and we left it at that. I am not sure where Jack got his version of events.

That was it, nothing more happened that night against Poland, the Irish team won 3-1 and looked to be doing fine without me, which was it. Then however Jack's book comes out a few years after the Euro's and in it he says I was drunk and trying to aggravate him. That made me feel worse about the whole thing, I am not sure why Jack felt the need to say that maybe he wanted to vindicate his decision to leave me out of the squad.

For Jack to tell me he did not have my number was ridiculous, it is so easy to get a number and if he wanted to speak to me he could have very easily arranged it, at the very least Jack could have said when he met me, 'Thanks for everything you did, I'm sorry you're not coming but I wanted to try different things in the build up to and at the tournament'.

I still might have been unhappy but at least it would have been something. Euro 1988 was the biggest thing to hit Irish football and after failing so close in World Cup qualifying in 1982 it would have been a fantastic experience to go along and play at a major tournament, which is what every player wants to do when they represent their country.

I know Jack is a hero but he was very lucky to get to Germany, who would have thought that Ireland would beat Scotland 1–0 and that Scotland would get a result against Bulgaria. I know this will sound like sour grapes but the teams that Jack faced were not as strong as those Johnny Giles and Eoin Hand faced in their campaigns.

It's funny but under Jack I never felt as part of the team as I did under Hand and Giles, with Jack everything was his way or the highway, Jack did all the talking but he would never say 'well done' or 'nice work' to me anyway, while for me Maurice Setters was a waste of time, I am not sure what he added to the set up.

Setters was only there as Jack's yes man if you ask me, he did not add much to training and never actually added much to the whole set up in my opinion. I always failed to understand his role within the Irish set up. Maybe I have tinted glasses but training under Giles and Hand was more intense than under Jack who felt that you should be doing all that with your club and it was not his job. His job it seemed was to pick the team.

Jack had his favourites, though and once you were in the clique he looked after you and make sure that you had everything you needed.

I was not in the clique and neither was Frank (Stapleton) or Liam (Brady), they were not his type of players. Being honest I found Jack big-headed and he was like that from the start.

The first time I met up with him was his first game in charge against Wales and we had a meeting before the game in the airport to train, because it was snowing in April; imagine, we actually trained in the hangers as we could not practice on the grass.

Jack told all present that no one would be left out of the squad for the next game. We all headed to the Airport Hotel that evening in buoyant mood after that chat with Jack and despite losing 1-0 to an Ian Rush goal the next day I was confident of my future with the team.

When the next squad was named for a game again Uruguay, I was left out despite being a Milk Cup winner with Oxford at the time, again there was no explanation, however Jack then rang me and told me to come over as a player had pulled out. I then featured in the squad again before being dropped for the away game against Scotland; I remember my mother was very upset over that decision, as again there was no explanation.

Jack, who in his book revealed that he was without me, opted to play my old friend Paul McGrath at right-back that night. I am not sure why he was without me though as I was very much available. Paul did not have a clue about playing in the full-back position and even said it at the time but in true Paul fashion he had a great game and Ireland won.

That was the beginning of the legend of Jack Charlton, he became a hero that night; it was a great result against a very good Scotland side.

As for me, I had fallen out of the picture at Oxford a bit and knew I needed games if I was to make it to Germany.

I had played just twice at the start of the 1987–88 season, although I had featured for Ireland in both games against Luxembourg I was afraid I would miss out on the Euro qualifiers and indeed the Euro's as well, so I opted to go out on loan. The chance to go to Leicester came at just the right time.

I needed games to get my fitness up; some players maintain a natural level of fitness, however I was not one of them and as I have said before, if I was not playing regularly I felt as if my game was falling apart. I wanted and needed to be playing.

Bryan Hamilton, the former Northern Ireland international, was the manager there at the time and when I met him he came across as a good man so even though I was dropping down a division I was happy to make the move, there was also the added plus that it was near Oxford too so I did not have too far to go.

I made my debut against Hull and thought I did well in that game, I ended up playing five games for the club, which went a long way to helping my fitness, however things did not work out there as Hamilton ended up getting the sack and David Pleat was appointed as his replacement.

I never spoke with nor heard from Pleat and at the end of the month's loan, Leicester decided not to renew my loan or make the move permanent so I returned to Oxford. Despite my brief spell there I had liked Leicester and thought I did well personally, although obviously results at the time were not great.

I came back to Oxford with my fitness back, however I still could not get in the side and knew I needed to move on if I was going to play. I was always a guy that liked to play, I would not have liked to sit on the sideline and pick up my pay packet – I wanted to play football. At least that is how I looked at it.

I liked playing under Maurice Evans at Oxford, he was a nice man but was very quiet. The same could not be said for his right-hand man, Ray Graydon. Ray was of the same mould as Ron Saunders, in fact he had been part of the Aston Villa team under Ron and he liked his football played in the same way. He was a fan of the long ball and I remember having many a row with him, not many of the lads liked him at the time but that said I was out of the team anyway and Maurice had gone out and signed another right-back so I knew my time was at the club was coming to an end. I handed in a transfer request and Maurice told me that Harry Redknapp wanted to sign me at Bournemouth.

In December 1987 I ended up moving back down to Division Two this time to Bournemouth. I remember I made my way down there to talk terms and check the place out and without really thinking about too much I signed for them.

All that was on my mind was the Euro's. I was worried no end, I mean, I had not played for Ireland since the qualifying win over Luxembourg and had been left out of the qualifier with Bulgaria as well as the friendly with Israel. I knew my place in the starting line up was under threat, Chris Morris, who had being doing very well for Celtic had come into the team for the 5–0 win over the Israelis and at 23 youth was very much on his side, I was the wrong side of 30 at that time, did not have the pace I once had and needed to be playing to convince Jack I was still an option.

Jack wanted his players to be playing and that was what I planned on doing, Bournemouth were a mid-table Second Division side and Harry was an up and coming manager then. Redknapp was the sort of manager that liked you when you were playing well and while I thought I did okay, I did nothing that would have set the pulses racing. I did not have much interaction with him though to be honest, although you can see from his career that he had a good knack at spotting talent, sadly I think I was one of those basement bargain signings that did not work out.

Despite playing regularly for Bournemouth, there was nothing eye-catching in my performances but my fitness was definitely improving. I genuinely thought that as I was getting games and had a good track record with Ireland I might be okay for the Euro's squad. I had only played nine first team games before Christmas, including the two with Ireland but I had finished the second half of the season playing regular football. It was not enough however and I was left out of the friendly games with Romania and Yugoslavia, the emergence of Chris Morris pushing me to the sidelines. Then came the Poland night, by then anyway I knew I was not going, so I had started to deal with it as best I could. I was devastated and spent the whole summer drinking.

My career was now in free fall and I was slowly making my way down the divisions, the rejection by Ireland hit me hard and I would never be the same player. That summer I left Bournemouth after only about 20 or so games and joined Peterborough who were in Division Four. In fewer than 12 months I had gone from being a top-flight footballer to a Division Four player, it was like a plane crash.

When Peterborough came in for me, being honest I did not really want to go, despite my eternal wish to play football, my head was not right and I must admit looking back I think there was some part inside of me that had lost that bit of desire to play.

The experience with Ireland broke my heart and I needed time to heal myself. A summer of drinking had not helped one bit and though I could cope with it, I was never the same player after that, my game just went to bits although Peterborough did not know any of this. They would never see the best of Dave Langan, in fact bar the 18 months when I was injured and useless to Birmingham they got the worst of me. I had simply lost my appetite for the game however I had to make a living, I knew nothing else so decided to go down there and have a look. Everything seemed to be good and decent there so I decided to accept their offer and made the move.

That summer I remember having mixed emotions watching Ireland in Germany, I was delighted for the players, well those that got us there but I hated seeing Jack getting all the praise for getting us there. It was a two-way thing, I wanted Ireland to do well but I wanted Jack to fail for what he did to me.

I spent the first few days of the tournament in Ireland and being honest

I drank a lot. I spent most of that summer drinking. I was devastated and I saw drink as a way to handle the pain I felt. I was depressed and down, I resented the players that were over there but had done nothing to get us there. I went into my shell and kept myself to myself, speaking to no one only a bottle of whiskey.

My whole world crumbled, at Leicester and Bournemouth I still had something to offer, I wanted to get my fitness up so I could be a part of the squad, I had a purpose but after missing out on Euro '88 I had nothing, my confidence was gone.

I mean I had dealt with being rejected by Manchester United. I had overcome knee and back injuries. But I could not raise myself after the rejection by Jack, I am sure people reading this will think I should have gotten over myself and just got on with it, I could not though. I just lost my enthusiasm for the game I loved so much and I carried that with me to Bournemouth and Peterborough United, they never got to see the best of me, I let both clubs down and it hurts me even now.

Earlier I said I kept myself to myself, that is true to a point, however I must set the record straight on some points as my poor mother had a lot to deal with during that time. I used to get drunk and I would phone her and get emotional. I would cry and pour my heart out to her, often being so drunk I could not recall what I had said to her.

I know she knew I was on the drink at the time but she never said anything and I must have broken her heart during that time. It must have been awful for her; I put her through so much.

My time with Peterborough will never be remembered by anyone except me, I was shite for them and they deserved better. At least with Bournemouth I had played a few good games, I had made a decent debut for them against Manchester City and had at least tried but with Peterborough I cannot ever remember playing one good game.

Not only was I struggling with depression at the time, but my back and legs were not right either, Mick Jones was the manager of them then and being honest it was a poor team. We finished the season fifth from bottom and won just 13 games all season. Not that I helped them at all.

My footballing free fall culminated in one of my most embarrassing moments in football, it was May 1989 and we were playing Hartlepool at home at London Road. I had been included in the squad despite not being fully fit. I remember Jones telling me that I would not be needed and was just there to make up the numbers. Turns out that was not the case. I remember I was jogging along the touchline warming up and the fans were booing me when Jones said to me, get changed you're going on. I could not believe it, he had told me that I would not be needed and now here he was telling me that I was going to have to go on. It was a ridiculous situation, I knew I was not fit but he said just go on. I did as I was told, I was booed coming on and as you would have it within minutes I became the first substitute in Peterborough history to be substituted, an unwanted record I can tell you. I think I was even booed coming off, my hamstring had gone again.

Jones was a nice guy though and I don't think he realised how damaged I was when he signed me, it was a poor team to be in and my head was not right. The situation got a bit messy after that sadly, as Jones thought I had defied him and faked injury and tried to fine me. The PFA had to get involved and in the end I got my payment. That was my last game in League football, not the way you plan you will bow out when you are an apprentice cleaning boots, you imagine you bow out with your head held high fresh from scoring the winning goal in a Final, not as the sub that was subbed.

I had not planned on finishing my career in football so soon and did not have anything saved up for a rainy day. I got the insurance pay out from the PFA while Peterborough paid out the final six months of my deal, which was not a whole lot. That meant that I was forced to go on and claim social welfare. I will never forget that day as long as I live, there was a massive queue when I went down there and I remember everyone there seemed to know who I was.

They were taking the mickey out of me something else, it was very hard to take and I thought about turning around but I stuck it out, I had no choice I needed the money. I would have loved to have stayed in football and coached but my injuries meant I would not have been able to do that. I eventually reached the main desk and they were very helpful. I got the paperwork signed off and started my new life on £52 a week.

I did not want to sit around claiming dole, however, I was determined to try and forge a new life for myself and to work. I went for an interview with the Post Office and I remember having to do my first test, outside of a fitness test, since I left school back in Ringsend in Dublin. I was so nervous and messed it up, they told me they would be in touch but I knew I would not be hearing back from them. Again just like the social welfare office, I was paranoid and could see all the postmen looking at me and whispering as I walked past them. I felt like shouting at them how I needed to work to earn money for my wife and kids.

I eventually got a job delivering dry cleaning, I was earning £120 a week and stayed there for eight months before they folded, then I tried my hand at delivering milk but lifting the crates proved hard on my back and I was in constant agony. I only lasted three months there. I remember I saw a job advertised with the Peterborough Council for a car park attendant and part of the advertisement said 'Are you disabled?' I was unsure what that meant but knew that because of my back I was not up to much. I was told in order to apply I needed a green card. I went and spoke to my doctor and was referred to a specialist who told me that because of my back I was now considered to be disabled.

It was hard hearing those words and I felt like a complete failure but I tried not on dwell on it too much as I had a family to feed. I finally got the green card and applied for the job, there were 100 applicants for it and in the end I was very fortunate to get it. I had practically begged for the job and told them I would not let them down. It must have worked as I got it and stayed in that role for four years.

I then moved to become a beadle, which was an ancient role akin to a town crier or keeper of the keys that was within the Peterborough Council. I went for it and was offered the job on a Friday and started on the Monday. The new job meant that I had to move to the Town Hall to work. I did that role for a while before one of the assistants left the Mayor's office and he asked me to fill in and take over that role. I have been doing that now for nine years. It is a nice job and there are some good aspects to it. I often have to give history talks on the town hall so I make sure I know my history and study up for it. I am very grateful to have been given the chance to work and it has helped me appreciate a lot of things in life.

Joe Corcoran

Joe Corcoran, who was there the night that Charlton and Dave met at Lansdowne Road, reckons that Dave deserved to go to Germany in 1988.

'Pride, passion and commitment – These are the words I think of when somebody mentions Dave Langan.

'On the pitch Dave was a terrier. His enthusiasm and energy around the pitch had to be seen to be believed. Unlike most full-backs around that time Dave was very attack minded. He loved getting forward and to be involved in attacks, even more so than wanting to defend.

'Away from the pitch there was another side to Dave. While he may have been full of life and energy when he crossed that white line, Dave off the pitch was a shy and reserved kind of guy.

'In many ways he was like his father. Dave wouldn't be one to rush to be the centre of attention any more than his father would. Dave was a bad mixer. He was a lovely guy but he would almost want to know who was in the room before he would agree to go in. He was that shy.

'However when he got on the pitch he came alive. Playing football, and in particular playing for Ireland meant everything to Dave. When he pulled on that green jersey you could feel it and see it in his eyes just how much that jersey, and everything it stood for, meant to Dave.

'In my opinion Dave was badly treated by the FAI and no more so when it came to Euro '88. I think it's on record that Dave played almost if not all the qualifying games leading up to that tournament and for him not to be included in the squad was wrong.

'Inside the camp at the time it was common knowledge that a few players were taken to Germany that weren't fit and hadn't a hope of playing in any of the matches and for them to leave Dave at home, it was crazy.

'That was the lowest moment in Dave's career. I would see him from time to time after it happened and although he wouldn't directly tell you how he was feeling, you could tell how hurt he was not to be included in the squad.

'Nobody but Dave knows how he feels about that period in his life, but it was easy to see just how much of a disappointment it was. He played with such passion and pride in the Ireland jersey, and when that was taken away from him, on the cusp of the biggest tournament he would ever play in, it crushed him.

'Like many people who know Dave we have our stand out moments from his career. Looking back I would say his performances against France when Ireland played them at home during the World Cup qualifying campaign and when they played Argentina, stand out for me.

'His performance against Maradona in particular is fresh in my mind. It shows the calibre of player that Dave was that he could stand toe to toe with a player like Maradona and did not look out of place.

'Dave was also a deeply religious guy. In fact one of his pre-match rituals was to bring Holy water into the changing room with him and dab a little bit of it on him before he went onto the pitch.

'I think when people look back on the career of Dave Langan they will remember that he gave everything he had each time he stepped out onto the pitch. You couldn't question his desire, his will to win or commitment to each team that he played for. That is as fine a legacy as you could wish for.'

Chapter Nine

Homelessness

As well as dealing with the injuries, the drinking, the gambling, the poor decisions and the marriage breakdowns not to mention missing out on my children's lives, one of the toughest parts of my life came about six years ago when I was left homeless and living in the basement of the town hall.

For anyone that has ever had to endure having no home to go to in the evening, they will know the feeling of shame, depression and failure that torments you as you lie on a makeshift bed trying to figure out where did it go wrong? It is not a nice feeling when you know you have nowhere to go and that no one wants you.

Here I was, a former Ireland international who had played for some of the biggest clubs in England, had won the Milk Cup and yet I could not afford to even rent a bedsit. I had well and truly hit the bottom. At the time I had nothing, my second marriage had fallen apart and I had left home, any money I was earning was helping to pay the bills for my estranged wife and kids, however, I had nowhere to go.

Once again I had managed to mess things up and in the end I got a small camp bed, the ones that you use when camping and set up shop in the basement of the town hall. It was a fold-up bed and not the most comfortable, although needs must. That bed certainly did not help with the back problems I experienced then and now.

A few of the lads I worked with knew of my situation and they kept my secret. I would work late in the evening, at that time I was working a lot of extra hours, some times my day did not finish until about 11pm which suited. When I was finished I would head downstairs to the basement, pull out my camp bed and a few blankets that some lads had given me and lie there thinking about my life.

Lying in that bed was the hardest thing not just for my back but for my well-being, I would think about everything, absolutely everything that had happened in my life and go over it many times during the night. Any sleep I did get was fitful, I never felt rested. Because it was an old building and I was in the basement, as well as the noises in my head I also had to listen to every noise that made its way through the building.

I often felt as though there was someone down in that big dark basement with me.

At 5.30am every morning the cleaners would come in to start their morning work and that was my alarm, I would get up and thankfully there was a shower in the basement, so I would wash, make myself some breakfast in the kitchen and then be ready to go for the day.

On my days off I would walk the towpath, go for a few drinks and watch a game. I was lucky in that I had an access card so I could come and go as I pleased.

It was very hard at that time; I know I was very depressed. I did not want to talk to anyone especially my family. I told them that I was in digs at the time and had no landline installed yet to talk to them, I used to text them to ring me on a payphone.

I tried to convince them that everything was okay but I think they could tell that something was up with me. Of course when I had a drink in me I would break down and just cry down the phone without making any sense, it was a tough time for my mother and sisters.

I then told a form of the truth in that I said that I had left home and I was living in a lovely room in the town hall, I did not want to hurt my mother any more than I already had. So I omitted to tell them that the lovely room I had was actually a store cupboard.

It actually crossed my mind a couple of times to pack in my so-called life in England and return home to Dublin. I remember one trip home, I went as far as looking at housing schemes in the city and was about to submit an application when the guy there told me there were thousands on the list and it would be a while before I got one, so that put me off. I also headed down to the dole office to sign for forms but in the end I decided that my life, as bad as it was, was in England and at the very least I had a job there.

If I had gone home I would have ended up living with my mother back in Ringsend with no friends about, everyone I had known as a child had moved on.

It all eventually came to a head as I got found out when someone told on me and the chief executive of the council said I could not go on living in the basement and that they would help me find some digs.

Another person who helped me around that time was Terry Conroy, the former Stoke and Ireland international. Conroy was working for the FAI at the time and he came up to see if I was okay.

Conroy actually gave me some money; a couple of hundred quid to help me get sorted with my digs. I was delighted and fair play to Terry, he was as good to me as anyone I had known through the years. I told my family that I had new digs and had managed to get a phone in so they could call and speak to me. It was like a massive weight had been lifted off me.

One of the shining lights during that time was the weekend training sessions I did with local kids, it was an opportunity to see my son and daughter too and I really enjoyed spending the time with them. It was also a buzz being back in football and training those 20 plus kids, including my own children gave me a real good feeling; it was the highlight of my weeks in those dark days.

Thankfully my kids never found out where I was living at the time.

The FAI, via Terry, kept in contact with me, Terry was great to keep in touch, I remember him driving down from Stoke to see how I was one time. He told me to meet him at the Great Northern Hotel that was near the railway station, it was close to my digs at the time and the landlady gave me a lift over.

When I saw Terry he came over and gave me a big hug and I just started crying in his arms, I was overcome with emotion and was grateful for the help they had given me. Terry would often give me a couple of quid to get back and he kept in contact with me.

Ray Houghton

While they might have different versions of events, Dave and Ray Houghton both agree that 'Langy' is one of the people who helped put the ball in the English net. Dave recommended Ray to the FAI, who listened for a change and the rest as they say is history. Ray recalls his memories of his time with Dave on and off the pitch.

'My relationship with Dave started when I moved to Oxford in 1985. Dave was the resident full-back at the time and I played on the right wing, so in a way we were partners in crime on the right-hand side of the team.

'Dave was great to play with. He loved going forward. For me that was Dave's biggest strength, that and his ability to cross a ball, which was second to none. He could stick the ball wherever was best for the striker and worse for the defender. It was something to watch.

'It has been mentioned that Dave was ahead of his time as regards his style of football, however, it is true.

'Dave would fit in so well if he were playing football today. He was a modern right full-back in the 1980s. He defended when he needed to but his first thought was always to get forward. He never stopped wanting to get on the ball.

'Off the field Dave was a lovely guy to be around. He wasn't a larger than life character, just a guy who went about his business in his own way. He loved having a laugh and a few bets on the horses from time to time. He kept himself to himself, but that was just Dave, a shy, quiet guy at heart.

'He wasn't above giving each player in the Oxford squad a nickname and I was no different. While John Aldridge was 'Jimmy Greaves' I was 'Mac'. If you got a nickname from Dave then you were doing something right.

'Dave played a crucial role in helping me play for the Republic Of Ireland. We were playing Aston Villa in the League Cup at Villa Park and Jack Charlton was at the game. Jack and Dave had a conversation and Dave happened to mention to Jack that I was available to play for the Republic. The rest as they say is history.

'It was tough on Dave that he didn't make the squad for Euro '88. At the time there were a few players like Dave and Mark Lawrenson, who missed out due to injury, that didn't make the final squad. It's unfortunate, as he would have made a big impact had he been there. Sometimes that's just the way it goes. I know a lot of the fans wanted Dave there. But sometimes life doesn't deliver what you want.

'While some people may have seen Dave at lower points in his life I never really saw Dave badly affected by drink. In my own experience it would only be when we would have to fly off for matches that Dave would have a drink.

'Dave had a huge fear of flying, which didn't help as he was a professional footballer. Before a flight Dave had a couple of drinks to calm himself down but that would be it. One time Dave was so on edge that he grabbed my hand as we were taking off so tightly and wouldn't let go.

'I know Dave had some off the field problems that he found hard to deal with. I know his family life was up and down at various times during his life. Dave is an emotional guy and can go from highs to lows sometimes but he never meant any harm by it that was just his nature.

'It's good to see that Dave has come through those bad times. I know that he still is held in high esteem by the players that he played with and we would never want to see anything bad happen to him. He is thought of too much for anything bad to happen to him.

'I think Dave will be remembered as someone who gave their all for his country. He loved his country and playing for Ireland so much. It meant everything to him and it showed in his performances. When he was out on the pitch he gave everything for the green jersey.

'He is still held in great affection by the fans because of that spirit he played with. They understood Dave was giving everything. They didn't ask for anything because they knew Dave was putting his all into whatever game he was playing.

'Dave was a gentleman to be around and some player to play with. He should be proud of the career he has had. It was a fine one.'

Chapter Ten

Three marriages, two divorces and three children

Along with my wife Dawn my mother is probably the greatest woman in my life. She has stood by me all these years, she has supported me during the good and bad times, especially the bad times and despite not having a lot herself she has always supported me financially too. It should really be the other way round, I should be the one supporting her but sadly I made some bad decisions and instead of her living her later years without a worry in the world, sadly she still had one worry left, me.

She is the best mother a son could ever ask for and I am pleased to have her. Sadly over the years I have lied to her and it is something I am not proud of, the only consolation I can find for myself is that I did it to give her peace of mind. My mother is an awful worrier and she is always praying, whether it is for me or my sisters, her Rosary beads are always out.

My mother is very religious and always goes to Mass, even now despite her age she manages to make her way down to Church and as she is very friendly with the priests there, if she cannot make it then she will get Masses said and candles lit. The religious side of my mother has rubbed off on my sisters, who also attend Mass regularly.

She used to spray holy water on my knees when I was home and I remember before every game I used to bless myself, which the lads at Birmingham found hilarious and used to rib me about.

She used to send me over a bottle of holy water every now and then; she thought it would help me avoid injury. I used to carry it with me on match days; the lads at the club used to give me a ribbing over it, one particular game, I cannot remember who exactly we were playing, Billy Whitehurst came up to me.

Whitehurst was a big burly striker, built like a brick outhouse, who struck fear into most defenders he played against. I actually remember Mick McCarthy and me chatting about a clash that was coming up between Oxford and Man City and Mick started chatting about Whitehurst, he told me that one time he was up against him and he said he would let him know he was in a game, so he went in hard on him only for Whitehurst to turn around and tell him, 'is that all you got?' Mick just thought to himself, 'Jaysus I'm in a game now!'

Anyway this particular day Whitehurst came up to me and asked me what was in the bottle, I told him it was holy water but he would not believe me and kept going on about it, eventually he just took the bottle and drank it. He actually thought it was vodka.

Whitehurst and I were actually good friends while we were together at Oxford and I used to drink with him; while he was a nice chap he would start a fight in an empty saloon with a drink in him. Me, Billy and Mick Moore would often head out after a game for a few, but no one ever approached us they were terrified of Billy.

My mother had been a big influence on my career and I don't think she would have been too happy to know the drinking and the gambling I did throughout my career. One of the hardest things about telling my story was realising that my mother would learn things about me that she never knew, things that I kept from her to avoid worrying her.

I am in a better place now in my life thankfully and that means she had less and less to worry about with me although that does not stop her. She gets on great with my wife Dawn and thinks the world of her. However, most people who meet Dawn like her, she is that kind of person. My sisters, who are an important part of my life, also think highly of Dawn and that has made being with her even easier than it already is.

I suppose it is not really common knowledge but I also have a brother, Billy, obviously those close to me would know about him, but outside of that it's not really something that I talk about. Sadly Billy has special needs and sadly we do not really have a relationship with each other. Billy is 58 and has spent most of his life in a House for people with Special Needs in Blackrock. My sisters bring him to my mother on a Friday to spend the weekend at home.

As you would expect as a child, I did not really fully understand what was wrong with Billy, I knew we were different but I did not know why. I was obsessed with playing football and Billy loved to listen to music. I used often hang around the house with him and put on records for him but we did not do a lot of things together. My dad was great with Billy though and he found the time to spend with Billy and me, not to mention the girls. I suppose growing up I was too obsessed with football to really pay too much attention to him and then I left home at a very young age so we never really developed an adult relationship. I often think it is sad that we did not have a relationship but I do love him.

Billy was mad about my Dad however and my dad was great with him, he would cut his hair and give him baths, it must have been hard for him but he never said anything. He loved Billy, but back then they were different times than they are today. When Dad died we all took it very hard, especially Billy. It was a big loss for us all. My father was a quiet man, a bit like me in a way and he hated attention or being the focus of attention.

I guess my father and I were very similar in many ways, and he was a fantastic influence on me. I used to love asking him after a match how I had played and he was always honest in his assessment, he never sugar coated it for me, If I had played well I got the credit, if I did not then he would tell me where I went wrong.

I know my father was disappointed when my first marriage broke up, like my mother he was a religious and traditional man. While there might only be a stretch of water between them, Ireland and England are very different in some respects. Over in Ireland, I know it's different nowadays, back then there was no such thing as divorce and given our Catholic upbringing there was no easy way out. If a marriage wasn't working and the couple were unhappy then they were just expected to either put up with it or separate.

While divorce is hard on two people, it is even harder when there are kids involved not to mention a religious family. My first marriage to Mandy only lasted a short spell however the split was still very upsetting and very hard on all parties. The whole episode was made that bit harder by the fact that there was a small baby involved. Elliot was only a baby when I left Mandy and it left a deep scar with me, I hated leaving him and even now feel guilty over it. However Mandy and I were not suited as a couple and we would have made life miserable for each other and for him had we stayed together. I struggled to show my emotions at times, unless of course there was drink involved and I think that Mandy thought I took the whole divorce in my stride, that was not the case though, it broke my heart seeing my marriage fall apart. Coming from a good religious background, I knew my family would have frowned upon what was going on. My mother and father would be missing out on seeing Elliot growing and also have to live with the shame of telling people that my marriage was over.

I had to think of Mandy and me though and not my family. It used to break my heart the few times, it was only a few times, that I took Elliot down to Birmingham and I remember when I would drop him back up I would be devastated, weeping in the car. Neither Mandy nor Elliot ever saw that and I suppose I should have opened up more to them but I did not know how to handle the situation. I was a still a young man and I was very naive.

Throughout my life I have had a lot of regrets, things that while I cannot fix now I would have loved to have had more foresight at the time and thought more about. One of those regrets was when I was in Oxford and we made the Cup Final. At the time I was elated to be in the side, even though it was so close to the Final and managed to arrange for tickets for my sisters to come over. Evans only told me on the Friday as he was a gentleman and I had pushed him into it, I was thinking of getting my sisters sorted to come over and was panicking to try and get them sorted.

A short while after the Final I got a letter that brought me right back down to earth, it was from Mandy telling me that Elliot had gotten very upset when he saw me on the television at Wembley. I had never sent tickets to them. I did not even bother to send tickets down to them, I should have but it slipped my mind at the time with the euphoria and the excitement not to mention the panic trying to sort my sisters out. I know it was silly at the time and would have only taken a second to arrange, even now when I think about it I realise it was a selfish thing to do, but at the time I did not even know I was playing and it was not until three days before the game that I found out but even as I read these words I know it is not good enough.

I must say that despite our differences, Mandy and I did manage to produce a wonderful son, Elliot and for that I am grateful. I am very fortunate that despite not really being around or being an influence on his life, Elliot has turned into a fine young man, credit for that must go to his mother and I am very proud of him. I know I let him down and I cannot hide from that no matter where I run to but I am glad he is a fine young man.

I met my second wife Debbie Brown while I was injured and on crutches. It was 1981 and I had just had my first knee operation, my first marriage to Mandy was over. I was in Birmingham while Mandy and Elliot were in Derby. I would still see Elliot when I could, but I suppose I wanted to meet someone and get my life back on track a bit. I was disappointed with the way my first marriage had turned out although I realise now that we were way too young to have got married like we did.

Mandy and Debbie were very different really. Unlike Mandy who was familiar with the Derby scene through her uncle Roy McFarland, I met Debbie through one of my other great loves at the time, gambling. Debbie would not have been familiar with the football scene and certainly would not have been down around the ground, she worked as a hairdresser.

I was with a fellow by the name of Tony Evans at the time, a striker with Birmingham and a lovely fella. We were heading into a bookie shop to put a bet on and there was a hairdressing shop beside it. I suppose if you took the bookies' part out of it you could describe it as a romantic meeting, as she took a look at me and I took a look at her, our eyes meeting.

One of the hairdressers she worked with came out and I asked her to do me a favour and ask that girl to go out for a drink with me. I called her that night and it developed from there.

It turned out that she lived near where I was staying at the time, which was with Gordon. We would see each other a couple of times a week, it was all very relaxed I suppose. She was a couple of years younger than me. We did the things normal couples did, we went to the pictures, went for meals and we went out for drinks.

She was a lovely girl and we really got on well, likewise I got on well with her family so everything looked to be going good. The only problem between us at the beginning was that Debbie was not overly fond of me drinking, I was out injured and she thought I was an idiot for drinking. She was too young really to do too much about it but it could not have been easy for her at the time. She was very patient with me though.

Debbie was with me when I moved to Oxford and we lived in a flat for a while down there. We actually got married down in Bournemouth before we settled in Peterborough; we were happy for a few years together but started to drift again. I was not the easiest to be around to be honest and struggled being out of football.

I left a few times but always came back until one time I just left for good. Our income and lifestyle had changed dramatically and it was hard to take, I had gone from being a professional footballer to being a car park attendant on about £10,000 a year without any real warning or preparation. It was hard for me but it was also hard for Debbie too, she went back working, she worked in Gap for a bit. I was still struggling to grasp the fact that my career was over and I could not play football anymore, I joined a team called Stamford in non-League football.

That was a humiliating experience and I should not have done that. Players from other teams would laugh at you and take the piss. They had no respect for you or what you had done in the game, I ended up playing for a pub team and I had nothing left at this point. I knew I should have just given up, but as always all I just wanted to do was to play football.

That was all I ever wanted, if I had not played football I am not sure what I would have done, being honest I would have probably ended up on the dole back home. I did not have any real warnings that my career was going to end, I was still only 32 years old and I had come back from serious injuries before so it really hit me hard. I did not know how to make the adjustment from playing to being told I could not play and however hard I found it to make the adjustment, I think Debbie found it that bit harder.

My second marriage to Debbie lasted a lot longer than my first but sadly the outcome was the same. Debbie and I had over 20 years of marriage together and again I was lucky to be blessed with wonderful children, Callum and Leah. Callum was born in 1989 and Leah arrived two years later and I can tell you like Elliot they have turned out to be fine children. The fallout from the second marriage was harder as it had lasted longer and I was around a bit more when they were growing up.

I suppose in the beginning I was not around a lot as I was working full-time during the week and playing non-League and pub football on weekends. Neither Leah nor Callum knew me as Dad the footballer. I had finished playing by the time they were little so they never really knew the good life that we had, although that said they were still looked after very well and never went without anything.

I used to have a good relationship with both Callum and Leah although Callum was a bit shyer so I spoke more with Leah.

Sadly these days there is not as much contact with each other and I miss them, they were good kids and deserved better. A lot of this is down to me once more, I had started to build a relationship with Leah after the whole split up with her mother and she had been around to meet Dawn, and they had seemed to get on well, so I was naturally happy.

Then just as things were starting to get better I managed to mess it up. Leah was competing in the Cancer Research Race for Life and wanted me to come down to watch her run. I was excited and delighted, of course I got my days mixed up and ended up missing it. I was so angry with myself and I knew I had blown it. I recently found out that Leah is in Africa doing some charity work, which is a great thing to do. Hopefully one day I can try and make things right between us all again.

Leah and Callum are lovely kids though and again I have to give credit to their mother. Despite loving all my children I was never the best of fathers, I don't know, it just never worked out for me I suppose. I did try but I suffered too much from depression not to mention injury to really appreciate what I had. It does hurt me that I don't see them but I cannot change that, I know though my door is always open to them and if they called tomorrow I would welcome them in with open arms.

I was with Debbie for 20 years but I think I made her life very tough for a lot of them; I was difficult to live with especially when I finished playing football. I was not happy in myself and I would say deep down Debbie was not either. I should have tried more but it is too late now to change all that.

The solicitor at the time of the divorce tried to make out that I had strayed during our relationship and I can tell you now that was not the case. My marriage had officially ended in the July and it was the following January before I got together with Dawn. At that time I was out of the marital home, in fact I was not even in a home, I was living in a basement in the town hall and we were separated. I had gone back at the Christmas to try and work things out but we both knew it was not going to work and that was the end of that sadly.

I got lucky with Dawn, we were both that bit older and wiser, although people might argue about how wise I actually was. She was a very stable woman and very kind and giving. That said I do hope Debbie is happy, as she deserves to be. I never gave my marriages with Mandy and Debbie a proper go, I was moody and hard to be around but I am a lot more comfortable and relaxed in myself these days.

As I said before, while my knees and back are painful, my life in general has improved a lot over the last few years and in a way I am happier than I have been in a long time. I finally seem to have settled down and faced up to a lot of things. I am a different married man these days.

My marriage with Dawn has really helped me start to enjoy the little things in life again and with a step-granddaughter on the way, the house is a busy place. Dawn has been such a good influence on me and I am so glad that I met and married her. She is a wonderful woman and without her I don't know where I would have ended up.

I am also getting in touch again with a lot of guys I knew during my playing days. Getting back in touch has been great and I have really enjoyed catching up with them and reminiscing about the old days. This is mainly down to a testimonial/benefit game that my old club Oxford organised for me in July 2011; the game was a shared night with former Oxford legend Joey Beauchamp. Like me Joey, who was a fine player in his day, has fallen on hard times as he struggles to make the adjustment from player to nobody.

When the idea of a benefit game was first mentioned to me I was, despite being in dire need of the financial benefits such a game would bring me, sick to the stomach. I had not been back to the ground in years and to be honest I was embarrassed about going back there; for me it really was a case of how far you can fall. I was not sure how people would react to me and if I would feel welcome or not.

So much had happened since I had played at the club, I had gone on to work as a car park attendant, I was registered disabled, I had suffered homelessness. I honestly thought everyone would laugh at me and think I was a fucking eejit for how my life had turned out. I had made a fool of my life and now I was expecting fans to help me to get by, it was hard to deal with.

When the idea for the game was first mooted Buildbase were the club's sponsors and they invited me down as a guest to a game against Cambridge. At half-time they wanted me to go onto the pitch and wave to the fans and I said to them, 'I cannot do that', I was too nervous. Eventually they talked me around, I think Mick Moore had a big part to play in that, I remember thinking to myself, 'Ah shit' before I headed out at half-time.

The reception I got though was amazing, they all gave me a standing ovation it was unreal and I was overcome with emotion. These fans remembered me, I could feel the lump building in my throat, it was a great feeling.

From there the benefit game started to take shape and a guy called Jeremy Hockley got involved and suggested we do a joint game with Joey Beauchamp, who had also fallen on hard times. I was delighted and agreed. After that initial contact I did not hear anything for about three to four months and I remember speaking to him about February when he told me they were having some technical problems but that it was going ahead.

The game was initially scheduled to take place in May, at the tail-end of the season however for reasons I am not sure about, Jeremy was forced to pull out and eventually my old friend Mick Moore and the chairman stepped in to take over the arrangements.

It was eventually decided that the game would take place in July, on 8 July 2011. The coverage was great, the local press and radio were back in contact and it was nice to feel like I had an opinion to give again. There were loads of letters and support on forums, it was really great to hear from so many fans who remembered me.

Denis Smith and my old boss Jim Smith were both lined up to manage different XI's with a host of former teammates and lads I played international football with taking part, my old friends Bobby McDonald and Trevor Hebberd played as did Ray Houghton, John Byrne and Mick Harford. It was great to see so many players I had known. My team, managed by Jim, were called Langy's Golden Oldies while Joey's team were called Joey's Promotion Team, it was a good night and a good game, Joey's team just beating us in a seven goal thriller.

Sadly for me I could not play in the game although it was great to be able to kick-off the game before limping off to the sidelines to watch. I would have loved to have been out there down tearing up and down the right wing. It was great to know that even though I had not seen these guys in years that they remembered and even respected what I had done in the game. It was a fabulous evening and I thoroughly enjoyed it. It's funny, there I was thinking people would not remember me and they did, it was me who had forgotten really.

I think the fans enjoyed it too although the audience was affected by some terrible weather not to mention Silverstone which was on that weekend but it was good night and I cannot thank everyone enough for helping arrange it and organise it. A lot of work went into the night.

It is funny but all these years I have been trying to forget Dave Langan the player but no matter what I do, people surprise me. I remember one time I was sweeping the floor after a wedding at the town hall and this guy came up to me and said, 'I think you are Dave Langan'.

Normally in these circumstances I would often say no, he is my brother my name is Frank but he seemed like a nice guy so I said, 'Yes I am'. He just said to me, 'What are you doing sweeping floors, I remember you as a great footballer?' What could I say to him? There was no point going through it all again, so I responded, 'It's my job, I have to earn a living' and that's the way it is.

More often than not nowadays I tend to use the name Frank Langan, when people ask me am I Dave Langan I tell them no. I feel as though Dave the player is a thing of the past and that Frank is the here and now and the man who has to pay the mortgage, has to work and has to battle the injuries that football inflicted on Dave.

But I was wrong, people did want to know how I was getting on, People did not mock me or judge me; they remembered me. I was only too happy to fade into the background and forget everything.

Not only was the game a great way to help me remember my footballing roots, it was also great to get in back in touch with so many of the lads I used to play with. Shortly after the game Dawn and I went for dinner with Trevor Hebberd and his girlfriend and it was great to catch up properly and talk about the old times, it is something we will do again. I am also back in contact with Bobby McDonald, who I was great pals with during the footballing days, at the time of writing this I was due to meet up with him and I am really looking forward to that catch-up.

One of the best reunions of them all though was getting back in touch with Mick Moore and his wife Sandra, they have been such good friends over the years and it was great to meet him and chat with them at the game.

Fan, work colleague and friend: Mick Moore

Former Oxford head groundsman Mick Moore was a fan even before he got to know Dave and 26 years on that friendship is still strong.

'Before I joined Oxford United in 1985 I had the privilege to watch and appreciate Dave Langan as a football fan. Perched in the stands I marvelled in wonderment at this guy from Ireland tearing down the wing like a man possessed. It was a joy to behold for anyone who watched him play.

'Dave was unlike any other full-back at that time. He was like a modern full-back. Back then full-backs rarely got up and down the wings. Their job was to defend. Nobody told Dave that. He was more of an attacking threat than a defender. That was Dave though, a bundle of energy that could not be contained.

'The one feature of Dave's play, aside from his amazing work rate, was his ability to cross a ball. He had the knack of curving the ball towards the goalkeeper then away from him in the same movement. It was the best display of pin-point crossing that I have ever seen. It must have been horrible to defend against, but that was the talent and ability Dave had.

'When I linked up with Oxford I got to know the man behind the footballer. Dave in many ways took me under his wing and guided me when I first started. He was a bundle of fun back then. He, like the rest of us, enjoyed the nightlife.

'He was also very popular with the ladies. While a few of us could expect Valentines Cards on February 14th, it was Dave who got the most. Perhaps it was his Irish charm that attracted the ladies.

'While he was in some ways a reserved character Dave could be great fun to be around. One of his favourite things to do was give nicknames to every player in the squad. John Aldridge was called 'Jimmy Greaves'. It always gave us a giggle when we would be out having a drink and Dave would say, 'Jimmy Greaves had a great game today,' people passing us would look at him as if he had two heads. Again that was Dave he loved a laugh and a joke.

'While a few people say that Dave had a drink problem, I for one, rarely saw it. The only occasions I would see Dave wanting a drink, aside from going out, would be when he had to fly. You see Dave had a huge fear of flying and the only way he could calm his nerves would be by having a few drinks before take-off.

'I know that he went through some off the field problems, including some marriage problems, but I never thought Dave had a drinking problem. Perhaps he just hid it well.

'Sometimes I would see Dave get down on himself from time to time. I would notice Dave walking past and he almost looked like a lost little boy at the time. No more so than when he was dropped from the Ireland squad.

'That was probably the lowest moment of his career. I was at the game when Jack Charlton dropped him. Dave got me a ticket for the game, but after the game was over he headed back to his Ma's house and left Niall Quinn to look after myself and another friend.

'It must have been tough for Dave as he was one of the mainstays in the team at the time. He also played a huge role in bringing Ray Houghton and John Aldridge into the Ireland squad, which people shouldn't forget.

'We have remained friends to this day. I helped organise his testimonial early in 2011. It was a great night, even though Dave had to share it with another player, which took the edge of it somewhat, it was still a well-deserved night.

'One thing that struck me when we had the testimonial for Dave was the regard that the ordinary fans still have for him. They regard him as a hero. Be it from scoring a never to be forgotten goal against Pat Jennings and Arsenal, or him tearing down the wing, the fans took Dave to their heart and kept him there.

'Even the new staff at Oxford came out to wish Dave well at his testimonial. That is the kind of impact he had on the club, as a man and as a player. He treated everyone with respect and that respect was afforded right back to him.

'It was so good to see Dave when he got married to his present wife Dawn. That day Dave was beaming from ear to ear and you could see he was genuinely happy. It was a huge contrast to the previous few years. Dawn has been a rock, and has made Dave as happy as he deserves to be.

'For me I value the friendship that I have with Dave to this day. We often went on holidays together and we forged a deep bond and friendship. In many ways I am indebted to Jim Smith for bringing Dave to Oxford, because without Jim, Dave and I may never have met.

'Jim saved Dave's career and for that he deserves a lot of credit. At the time Dave was troubled by back injuries. Jim took no notice of that and signed Dave. Some people may have wondered what Jim was doing, but Jim knew what Dave could offer and snapped him up.

'Dave was in many ways a fragile hero. He passionately loved his football and gave it everything he had. He may have got down from time to time, but who hasn't? He was a cracking player and more importantly he was a top bloke and to this day my friend.'

Chapter Eleven

Too much trust

The game nowadays is littered with agents and representatives all of whom offer advice to players from their contracts and investments to commercial opportunities, however, when I was a youngster signing my first professional deal with Derby I took what I was told I was getting. Likewise when I went to Birmingham Colin Murphy effectively told me not to hamper my chances of a move by asking for silly money, talk about having my back. I was very naive in those days and trustful of the advice I was getting even though it was coming from people that were not thinking about me at all.

Even now when young lads head over to England, they are often becoming millionaires on the back of their professional deal at the age of 17 or 18. It's huge money and to be honest it sets them up before they even really kick a ball. There was nothing like that in my day, you got £20 a week and you had to make it last, it was buttons really and I remember borrowing from local kids in the area of a weekend.

That said during my career while I did not earn the money that footballers nowadays earn I still managed an above average wage but never had anything to show for it. I think if I had someone that I could have trusted to guide me I would have fared a lot better.

Like now but probably on a smaller scale, football was full of hangers on, people who liked to be seen out with footballers having a laugh and drink.

At Derby and Birmingham it was no different there were always people out tapping you for drinks and a couple of quid. They assumed that you had it and that you were rich. That was not quite the truth although a lot of players, myself included, liked to let on we had more than we did. It was a social thing and people took advantage of our pride.

Drink and gambling cost me a small fortune – throughout my career when I was drunk, people used to ask me for money and being the fool I was I gave it to them and never got it back, when I got tips I put money on them and generally lost.

During my time at Birmingham, especially when I was out of the game for a long time and constantly hitting the bottle, I was a sucker for companionship and would drink with anyone that was happy to do so. I remember giving an apprentice whose name I cannot remember now for the life of me, a loan of £100 and never seeing it again. £100 was a lot of money back then although there might have been a sense of karma about it as I had done something similar to Colin Todd when he was kind enough to loan me some money.

People you meet out always assumed that because you were a footballer you had money and I never learned from any of my lessons. Because of my shy nature and a penchant for heavy drinking, I was always an easy target. I might have been the life and soul of a party with drink in me but the next morning I would be a mess. I would wake up from a night out and would have no idea where my money had gone. I could not keep track of what I was drinking and who was borrowing from me.

Whether it was from a night out or gambling, one time I arrived at training with £150 in my trouser pocket. Not even in a wallet just stuffed in there. I changed into my gear and did not pay the money any bother, when I went back into the changing room afterwards the money had been stolen from my gear. I was raging, someone had gone through my stuff and had found the money and taken it. It had to be someone from within the club, although to this day I have no idea who it was.

When I was injured and away from the club, I spent a lot of time drinking down in the local pub. As I was in there at all times of the day, I would be drinking with whoever was about at the time, I got to know the barman quite well there. The sad thing was, I was outside my normal circle. None of the players I was friendly with would be around. I often hung around with another player if he was injured and you would nearly be glad if someone was forced to spend some time on the sidelines, although you never wished it on them.

As I have said the club and players don't want anything to do with you when you are away from the ground injured, as the saying goes, out of sight, out of mind, I was certainly out of sight and I think I was out of my mind too.

When I left football, it was like being injured all over again. Lads I used to be able to get tickets off before suddenly disappeared, fellas I used to have pints with were suddenly busy – no one wanted to know me and I was very much alone. Think of it in ordinary terms, you have been in a job for 10 years, you know everyone around the office, you are popular and people stop by your desk for a chat and then one day you're called in and told you've been made redundant, get your stuff and leave. You don't get the chance to say goodbye to anyone and suddenly you are gone, chucked out and alone. How many of those people do you ever see again? How many of the people that dropped by your desk for a chat or that you had lunch or beers with stay in contact, not too many. It was no different in my case.

I found it all too much at times to deal with but I really learned a lot from that experience although by then it was too late as I had nothing for the hangers on to take from me. I was the sort of guy that drifted away from people especially if I was not in regular contact with people. I had a tendency to retreat into a shell and not bother people. Once football had finished for me I found it difficult to keep in touch with my former teammates. It was a confidence thing, I remember Charlie George used to walk into a place as if he owned it, I would walk in with my shoulders slouched and my head down as if I was afraid I was about to be kicked out at any minute.

I felt that football had turned its back on me, even though I was the one that had sunk into a shell, I expected everyone to still keep in touch with me. Sadly it does not work that way, after my appearance on the Joe Duffy show, former Shamrock Rovers star Mick Lawlor and Terry Conroy both got in contact with me to have a chat. Even after the benefit game in Ballyfermot I had drifted back into my life in England, I suppose at the time I was embarrassed, even though I was grateful for all the help. I could not help thinking back to the £100s I gave here and there and how they would have added up over time.

One of a small number of people I have always trusted was my old manager at Cherry Orchard, John Wilkes. John is one of the few people outside of my family who has been there for me all my life and I am very lucky to count him and Gerry Flynn as friends. Even now I regularly write to John and we keep in contact a lot.

John has been like a second father to me throughout my life but like a lot of other people who I have known in my life I had lost contact over the years, although thankfully enough we have re-established contact with each other in the last few years.

We regularly write to each other and the talk about football mainly, how Cherry Orchard are doing, Shamrock Rovers, the Irish football team and of course any problems each of us may be having, although truth be told more often than not John will help me with a problem I am having.

John was the one who told me that if I moved to Cherry Orchard he would get me a shot at playing in England. He was true to his word, he believed in me, probably more so than I believed in myself.

Of course as I battled my demons through the years one of the people I lost contact with was John and his reintroduction into my life came about in sad circumstances and ended up with a benefit night held by Cherry Orchard in Ballyfermot.

My father had just passed away and I had come home for the funeral. I was sitting in the church in Ringsend up at the front and I was sobbing, when I felt someone tap my leg. It was John. He said to me 'I'm sorry to hear about your dad'.

It had been years since we had seen each other, never mind spoken and it was very nice to see, despite the occasion. While we wrote to each other at the beginning of my time in England, that had stopped over the intervening years, mainly down to me.

John knew about my plight at the time, he heard from people about how things had turned out and as always, despite not seeing me, he wanted to help me. He told me that Cherry Orchard would do something to help me, and true to his word he got in contact two weeks later to tell me that the club were arranging a night in honour of me.

This was long before I would have the FAI benefit dinner, and while it was their way of helping me out it was also a gesture to show their appreciation for what I had done with them. The night took place in Ballyfermot back in 1999 and a load of my old Cherry Orchard teammates, including Tony Maher, Christy Bradley and John Byrne, the centre-half from the team and many more all turned up on the night, it was great to see them and we had a great catch-up.

It was great as well as my mother and three sisters also came along on the night so it was good for them to see lads I had grown up with although I think the star of the show might have been Paul McGrath, the reception he got when he came was unreal, the place went wild. It was lovely of him to come along and we had a good catch up, he was in good form that night. I suppose me and Paul share a lot of common traits, although he was by far the better player, demons have haunted us off the field.

I roomed with Paul once or twice for Ireland, at different times I roomed with Ray Houghton, Gerry Daly, who I knew from Derby and was lovely and Jim Beglin, but sharing with Paul was a different experience; he was so quiet you would hardly know he was in the room.

He was a great player though, he would be one of the best players I ever played with. He just seemed to have an extra gear that other players did not have, when he moved up a gear it was unbelievable and it really was poetry in motion, there was no way you could leave Paul out of the team. If a player ever got past you, you always knew that he would not get past Paul. It was a great comfort to have as a player.

Paul might have sent the crowd wild in Ballyfermot but that night was all thanks to Wilkes, who as I have said before was like a second father to me and he was always looking out for me and trying to help, the dinner being another example of him thinking of me. I have been very lucky to count John as a friend and even now I enjoy speaking with John and catching up and talking football.

John Wilkes

The feeling of respect and admiration is mutual with John who recalls Dave fondly, 'For me Dave Langan was a true Dub, and from the time that I first met him until now Dave has remained the same. I first met Dave when he was on trial for the Under-15 DDSL team. In the beginning Dave didn't really stand out in terms of star quality yet when he took to the pitch he showed us all what talent he had.

'At the time there were the likes of Frank Stapleton and Noel King who stood out. Dave was quite reserved but when he took to the pitch his talent shone through. Over time however Dave began to shine and slowly revealed himself to be an outstanding young prospect.

'Originally he started out playing in midfield and he flourished and looked a player of real quality. Indeed he could have spent his entire career in midfield and he wouldn't be out of place at any stage.

'As a player Dave had all the attributes of a top class player. He had great box-to-box ability, a tremendous engine room and to round it off he could score his fair share of goals. He was in many ways the complete player, and he worked himself into the ground. It would be a hallmark of Dave that stuck with him throughout his career.

'Before he went to England Dave was noted as a midfielder. It was never thought to move Dave from midfield but when he went to Derby County he converted to full-back and he flourished. All the skills needed to operate in midfield he used to tremendous effect.

'He had a natural instinct to get forward and that helped him when he moved position. Dave was always attack minded and wasn't content with being just a defensive full-back. Getting forward was one of Dave's best attributes.

'Off the pitch Dave kept himself to himself. He was an introvert and went about his own business without too much fuss. That was Dave. He just kept his head down and got on with things. When he signed for Cherry Orchard he was still very much in his shell. That shyness didn't stop him on the pitch. In fact he was anything but shy on the pitch and had no problem getting stuck in when it mattered.

'While his career was cut short I think that Dave's career will be remembered with tremendous affection by everyone who saw him play. While he was a little bit aloof, people were attracted to Dave. It maybe that he was just that little bit different although that said people felt comfortable with Dave.

'Fans could see themselves in Dave. He was hard working and tried his best every time he took to the pitch. Dave was an ordinary Dub, much like the people who came to watch him play. He had a swashbuckling style to his play that fans enjoyed.

'There was that ordinariness to Dave that fans gravitated to. Not like now where players and fans are so far apart, fans saw something in Dave that they had and they knew when he took the pitch for Ireland he would give his all.

'One of the reasons that Dave is held in such high regard by Irish fans is that he never forgot the ordinary punter or where he came from. While he may have played his club football in England he was a hometown guy to his boots and will be always remembered for his dedication for club and country.'

Chapter Twelve

A determined Irish fan helps me out

While I am now good friends with Con Meehan, I had never heard of him, met him or come across him before he set about highlighting my plight. Con was just an Irish fan who went that step further than any fan would ever go. His father Michael, who I have since met, was a big fan of mine who used to tell Con about how I played for Ireland. I was aware of the You Boys in Green forum and knew that some stories had been written before about getting a testimonial for me but nothing had ever happened.

The first contact between us was a text, and it developed from there. We eventually got to speaking terms and I suppose from there everything snowballed. I remember one of the initial texts from Con was about getting access to my pictures and trophies. Despite not really knowing him, I trusted him, after all he was trying to help me, and I did not have anything really worth stealing, so I let him. Con went down to my boyhood home in Ringsend and met my mother and sisters; I gave him access to the scrapbooks that my sisters had kept from when I first started playing football.

Con it turns out became a great friend and he has been great to my mother and sisters and we all think the world of him. He regularly pops down to my mother's home in Ringsend to see that she is okay and always checks in on me too, you would never think he is younger than us both. But he is a lovely fella and I am really glad to have met him and for everything he has done to help.

Con was not finished with just the scrap books and trophies, he went online to do more research about me and came across a forum run by You Boys in Green. He put a message up highlighting my plight and misfortunes. The response was unreal and he managed to get the full backing of You Boys in Green and between them all they pushed and pushed until something happened for me, they would not rest until they got something organised for me. It was very heart warming to know that these lads, these fans, were behind me 100 per cent.

YBIG and Con got Vincent Hogan of the Irish Independent to write a piece about me and that helped the cause even further. Vincent interviewed me for it and I must say it was an amazing piece, highlighting why he is regarded as one of the best Sports Journalists in the country.

They never gave up on me. They even got me on an Irish radio show called Live Line hosted by Joe Duffy. That experience in particular was one of the most emotional parts of the journey to the benefit dinner. I remember breaking down on the show. Con was there with me as was Phelim Warren and they thankfully were able to keep it together. Con spoke about the injuries I had suffered and my struggles. I just tried to be as honest as I could on the show, I was not bitter about what had happened, don't get me wrong I would have liked for things to have turned out differently but a lot of the time there was no one I could blame, only myself. I just wanted some help to get myself back on track and try and have a normal life.

Con and Phelim also met with Gerry McDermott and Mick Lawlor, I knew Mick. He had been a great striker as a kid and I remember him playing for Shamrock Rovers. There were only a couple of years between us, but he broke into the Hoops team very young. He also had been capped for Ireland a few times, although we had never played on the same Irish team, and was now employed by the FAI.

The meetings went well, Gerry was the media representative for the FAI while Mick understood football, the meetings were good and they understood and appreciated my plight.

The hard work eventually paid off as the FAI agreed to host a benefit dinner in honour. The date of the dinner was set for the 11 October, it was also agreed that I would be presented with an Irish legends award at half-time of the game between Ireland and Serbia. That game was the May before the benefit dinner and was also Giovanni Trapattoni's first game in charge.

Because it was the Italian's first game, there was a very good crowd, I remember then at half-time making my way on the pitch, the reception I got was lovely even though I can imagine a lot of people in the stands would not have known who I was and must have thought I had won a competition on the radio or something. It was nice to finally get some recognition though and even though it had taken a long time to happen, it was lovely. It was also great to get back on the field for an Irish match even in the unfamiliar surroundings of Croke Park although I doubt I would have been much use to Trapattoni if he had needed me. The trophy itself was a lovely gesture and sits proudly on the fireplace in my mother's house.

In the months between the award and the benefit night I was a mix of excitement and nerves. It was nice that people remembered me and wanted to help me but I was also nervous about who would turn up and how it all would go.

The night of the dinner itself, I remember we flew in, Dawn, and myself and stayed in the Burlington, which was lovely. A lot of people had confirmed they would be there; my family was going to be there, old teammates from my playing day in England and with Ireland, my old Cherry Orchard coach John Wilkes was there.

It was lovely to see so many familiar faces again, people I had lost contact with over the years and I have to admit I was overcome with emotion on more than one occasion.

I remember before the dinner, having a few drinks to calm me down, I was so nervous. There were a lot of people there, all of them for me and I must admit I felt inferior, I was terrified of facing them wondering what they would think of this footballer who had let everything slip away and now needed their help just to get by. The few drinks took the edge off me and gave me a bit of confidence. I managed to relax a bit although deep down that feeling of wasting everything never left. It made my stomach uncomfortable.

We had a great catch-up though and a chat and there were fans and former players everywhere, it was great the effort that people went to for me. My mother came down for it, as did my son Elliot, who flew over with his girlfriend and my sisters. I was delighted they all were there too for the dinner. I was also delighted that Elliot got to come over, it meant a lot to me.

I remember Ray Houghton giving my mother and me a big hug. It was really lovely to see them all again. I find it very hard to recount fully word for word the speeches that were made that night, there are parts of the night that are a bit of a blur to be honest as there was so much going on and so much attention on me. I had not had that much focus and attention on me in a long time and at times I nearly had to pinch myself and remind myself that all these people were there to help and that I had not wandered into someone else's party by accident.

MC for the night was the great Jimmy Magee, a legend in the world of sport commentary in Ireland and it was great to have him there, I knew his son Paul very well and like his dad he was a lovely fella too. I was very sad when I heard that Paul had passed away. Paul had been part of that great Cherry Orchard team and he was one hell of a striker for us that season, scoring loads of goals. I had met up with him when they had the benefit night for me in Ballyfermot and it was lovely to see him again.

His father Jimmy is always a lovely man, I remember my mother, who used to always listen to Irish matches on the radio or on TV, used to tell me that Magee always described me as like a greyhound. It was great to have him there.

I distinctively recall Eoin Hand and Liam Brady giving lovely speeches about me, Eoin spoke about the values I had as a player and the commitment I had, while Liam went on about me saying that I needed to be reined in at times, such was my enthusiasm and passion, and he even remembered me running up and down the pitch although thankfully he left out the words headless chicken. He managed to get the audience laughing when he cracked a joke about how I used to think I was a striker. That often appeared the case on the pitch I used to get that far forward.

It was very good of Liam to remember me in such a manner, especially as he was such a great player who had done it all. I would love to be able to see those speeches again, I think the actual dinner and speeches were filmed but I have never actually seen them, I must get in touch with the FAI about them, they are probably down in a vault somewhere.

A lot of my old club and International teammates and managers contributed to the night, I remember Niall Quinn gave a tour of Sunderland, there were signed shirts and John Wilkes gave away a ticket to Wembley.

I know this will sound very ungrateful and I don't mean it to be, but when I look back now I actually have mixed emotions about that night. While I am extremely grateful for the work of Con, You boys in Green and all the people who made it a night I will never forget, there is a part of me that feels that the FAI never really had my back on it and that they only did it because they had to, not because they wanted to. I know Gerry and Mick were great in helping out and arranging it but I am talking about the real powerbrokers in the FAI.

As I said I don't want to sound ungrateful and I am sure some people will see it that way but I have often thought about this and I genuinely think that the FAI only did it to get people off their backs. There was nothing untoward to me on the evening in fact the FAI were very nice to me on the night but you feel that if they had their way nothing would have ever happened.

The sad thing was they were doling out testimonials to players who were already millionaires yet were refusing to give one to a former player who gave everything for his country and ended up homeless; it beggared belief in my eyes.

Football Associations and club chairmen will always get grief, it is almost part of the culture of the game, the FAI have taken a lot of stick over the years but they did not always help it either, there was always a large entourage on any away game, there were always fights to ensure that the players had the best of facilities, Giles managed to change a lot of things, in a way he was the first big name manager that Ireland had and he was used to having the best of facilities at Manchester United and Leeds United. I suppose because the FAI needed him at the time they bowed a bit to his demands.

The FAI has always helped me a small bit over the years without ever giving me the payday that my 26 caps deserved. When I was homeless, Terry Conroy and FAI gave me a few hundred quid to help me get back on my feet, when they bowed to public pressure and the You Boys in Green campaign, they gave me a benefit dinner, again to help me out and while at times I am grateful for the support they have given me, let it be said they still don't make life all that easy for me.

I was not a millionaire footballer who was looking for a final pay day to set up a nice little nest egg for my family, I did not have a pot to piss in and I needed their help but not with the perceived attitude that came along with it.

While the FAI did their public part and arranged for the benefit dinner in my honour in my opinion they failed me afterwards in their treatment of me.

The benefit dinner was a great success, and everyone, me included, had a wonderful evening. What was particularly pleasing was that the money collected was going to help me sort out a house for Dawn and myself and would ensure that I at least had a decent roof over my head.

After the dinner the FAI and I met to agree on a payment plan for the money. At the time, Dawn and I were trying to buy a house and needed the money to get a mortgage from the Bank, so naturally we wanted the full amount. I even remember John Delaney, saying to me that he would do his best for us as he knew we needed the money at the time.

However the FAI would not agree to pay the money in full and instead agreed to pay a percentage upfront with the remainder of the balance to be paid at future dates.

We had agreed to buy a house in Peterborough and with the upfront amount were able to secure the mortgage. The house was not liveable at the time and needed a lot of repair work done, including new windows, so we agreed with the bank to take out a loan to cover the remaining amount of the benefit money due.

The FAI and I came to an agreement over how the balance would be paid to me and on the back of that the Bank were comfortable enough to give us a three year loan that was used to renovate the house.

It was the beginning of what on paper looked to be a relatively simple process for all parties but instead has turned into an ordeal for my family and me. From the very first payment, which the FAI forgot to pay, right up to now, it has been an ordeal to arrange payment of the lump sums.

After the first missed payment, my sister Audrey contacted the FAI and they advised that it would be sorted, it was, but sadly it took them until two months later to resolve it.

Since then, my sister has had to ring the FAI at least once a month, sometimes more, in order to get the payment sorted. It's not as if it is even the FAI's money so I'm not sure why there is an ordeal, the money was raised for me by supporters so there should not be the hassle there is.

They told us after the initial mess up that they would pay the money via direct debit on each scheduled date, however I know for a fact that never happened, Audrey and I would not have had to constantly chase if that had been done.

Each time either one of us gets to speak to someone we have to go through everything all over again, it is frustrating for me and Dawn, for my sister and for my mother who does nothing but worry about it. Not only that but it leads to overdraft and bank charges at my end which I have to cover.

The latest incident in October 2011, which the FAI told Audrey was a misunderstanding, forced my hand, I told Audrey to tell them that we would go the press and tell them the issues we have been having. The Finance person in the FAI told Audrey that they hoped it would not come to that and that they were working on getting the payment made. I was so frustrated with the latest events I ended up writing a registered letter to John Delaney asking him to sort this out once and for all. I am fed up with the bother each month.

As things stand I am in the final five months of the 36 and just want these to run smoothly so I can finish the loan and claim what was raised for me. A lot of what has been fed to Audrey and me has been lies, which have caused me no end of worry.

Even after everything that had gone on, starting with me being injured playing for Ireland to needing a public campaign and petition to get the benefit dinner, the FAI were still not willing to fully commit to helping me out. It makes it feel like they felt they bowed to public demand to give me the dinner and now they have shut the supporters up they moved on from it. I wish they had just paid the money over to me at the beginning and not kept it in their grasp for the last few years. It was like I was always going to be indebted to them for helping me.

A father's words transform Dave's life

Conleth Meehan was a key man in the campaign for the FAI to recognise Dave's struggles and what began as a quest to help out a hero of his father has ended up turning into a friendship.

'Basically I had grown up listening to my father speaking about Davey Langan, he would tell me about how much of a great player Dave was and how passionate he was about playing for Ireland. He also told me about the horror tackle that would eventually end Dave's career. However I was too young to have ever seen him play and aside from the stories my father told me I did not really know too much about him.

'I remember stumbling across the You Boys in Green website and posted a comment about Dave under a thread on the site, the response was amazing especially from the older lads on the forum. I could not get over how many people remembered Dave and how fondly they all recalled him. He was not just a hero to my dad; he seemed to be a hero to a whole generation of Irish fans.

'After much regaling of their favourite Davey Langan moments, the comments switched to the more serious matter of how Irish fans could help him. Phelim Warren, who was a massive fan of Dave and would have seen him in the flesh, e-mailed Vincent Hogan to see if there was anything he could do.

'We also tried to get in touch with Dave but failed, however two weeks after Phelim contacted Vincent, an interview appeared in *The Independent*, it was a great piece.

'I eventually got Dave's number and we began texting before eventually myself, Dave and Phelim had a chat about what we could do for him. As we talked about Dave's misfortunes it became more and more apparent that it was not up to us to help him it was up to the FAI.

'They were the ones that had turned their back on Dave when he needed them most especially as Dave's injuries were sustained playing for Ireland.

'We changed the focus of our campaign and began to lobby the FAI into arranging a testimonial for Dave. I went on Joe Duffy's Live Line show with Dave and the response was phenomenal, the momentum began to build and eventually we got a meeting with Gerry McDermott and Mick Lawlor from the FAI.

'They told us that testimonials were not granted any more and that the only real way they could help Dave was through the player fund, however that was never going to be enough to help someone making their way, especially someone not able-bodied.

'We continued to badger the FAI and I remember one of the key moments in our campaign was when Cathal Dervan did a piece on the back page of *The Star* about Dave's plight.

'Eventually the FAI wavered and agreed to hold a benefit dinner in the Burlington in October 2008, which as luck would have it, was just before the shit hit the fan, as I am not sure we would have gotten as far as we did.

'It was a great night, and while it was great to see Dave reunited with some of his old colleagues, I remember Niall Quinn bought a table that night, it was more important to see Dave get some cash together to be able to get a mortgage and buy a house.

'We have become really good friends since then, we text and talk quite a bit, I suppose as I've gotten to know Dave a bit more, one of the main things I learned is the difference between the professional footballers of nowadays and the 1980s. They really were different times, people tend to think that just because you were a footballer that you had it made, but it wasn't really the case.

'I don't think you could meet a nicer ex-pro, Dave loves to talk football despite coming across as someone who almost wants to forget his life as a player. He uses the name Frank nowadays to escape from his life in the top flight. It's unreal, he is so unassuming yet this is a man that played for some of England's biggest clubs and he's almost apologetic for it. Dave's a very trusting man and I think that led to him being burnt not just during his heyday as a footballer but throughout his life.

'The hardest thing for fans of Dave is that when you look at the players he played with and against, he measured up to them all and yet his name is almost missing from Irish soccer history except to those that are really clued in. It is sad to say but I think Dave just missed out on the gravy train, and who knows if he had made the trip to Germany in 1988 life might have been very different for him.'

Con and You Boys in Green were really good to me, I remember when the Vincent Hogan article first appeared in the paper, a guy I had known in Peterborough came into the town hall and put the brochure of the benefit dinner down in front of me and said to me that in all the years he had known me, he had never known I was a former footballer.

I never really realised how far down inside of me I had let the footballer go, I hated people commenting on how far I had fallen especially when I was working in the car park or sweeping the floor, I did not want their pity or their stares for that matter so I suppose I did not talk about my former life and just got on with my new life.

My life now is more settled, I have found a sense of meaning outside of football. I enjoy my time with Dawn, it's an easy life. My wife's daughter Victoria has just given birth to a lovely daughter, Takara while my sister Audrey's daughter Clare has also given birth to a son, who they have named Dave, after me.

Of course there are the worries that will always exist when you have suffered the injuries I have, but it's easier to get on with life when you have a good strong base. Telling my story has given me a chance to close a couple of chapters in my life that I needed to move on from and while I have enjoyed looking back at my life, there have been elements which have been painful. I feel at last that I have buried the ghosts of my past and now I can enjoy my future.

Chapter Thirteen

A family affair – Elliot, Dawn and his sister Audrey

A proud son – Elliot

'One of the earliest memories that I have of my father is him taking me to football games when I was a young boy. Every time we would be walking back from the game we would have a kick about with him being in goal.

'My one abiding memory from those games was when my dad would let me take a penalty against some of the bigger kids that were playing. I always remember the penalty spot been slightly elevated and more often than not I would send my penalty-kick high and wide over the bar.

'Despite my parents splitting up when I was very young I had a good relationship with my dad growing up. We would write to each other all the time. He would always ask how school was going, how I was getting on with my football and just being as good a father as he could be.

'He never missed a birthday of mine and would always send money in a card so I could treat myself, especially around Christmas time. In that sense I couldn't fault him. Despite been separated from us he always kept in contact and would try see us whenever our schedules allowed.

'While I was too young to see my dad play live I managed to get my hands on a number of DVDs of his career. The DVD that I saw of his Milk Cup performances still stands out for me.

'In many ways he was before his time. His commitment, the way he bombed forward and attacked was something few players did at the time. He put his heart and soul into every performance and watching those DVDs that passion came right through the screen.

'Like many people I still wonder why my dad never made it into the Ireland squad for Euro '88. It came like a bolt out of the blue. While he never did fully explain what happened you could tell how crushed my dad was by being left out of the team.

'It was a massive low in his career. Along with the bad injuries that he got throughout his career, not being picked for Euro '88 was one of the worst moments of his career. It was sad to see someone you love being that low.

'It was his battle with drink however that was the toughest thing we have gone through. While I didn't see much of him I could tell by the tone of the letters that he sent me just how low he was feeling. It was so sad to see him so depressed and down in the dumps.

'My dad didn't want to burden me with the problems he was going through. He wanted to shield me from what was happening. It was tough to see someone you love so much suffering so badly.

'I tried to help as much as I could. I contacted his former manager Jim Smith to see if we could do anything for my dad. He was and still is held in great esteem by the people he worked with and we all just wanted to see him happy and healthy.

'Thankfully he has turned the corner. The testimonial dinner that was held for him a few years ago was a turning point. I know that he was really touched by that night and the trouble that people went to be at the dinner, the likes of Niall Quinn and Ray Houghton, it really meant a lot to him.

'There was also a lovely piece done in the *Derby Telegraph* around the same time talking about my father and informing everyone how he was getting on. It proved what a good impact he had at the clubs he played for that people still want to know how he is getting on.

'I'm delighted to say that we have a good relationship at the moment. His marriage to Dawn has made him really happy and we are both in a good place.

We see each other a few times a year mainly when Derby are playing. We meet up, have a cup of tea and chat like any father and son would do. He still worries about me and asks how everything is going. What gives me the most satisfaction is having that time to meet up and just spend time with him.

'It was tough to see him during the really dark days. However, the way he bounced back and got past his problems gives me a great source of pride.

'I think when anyone looks back on my father's career they will all agree just what a good player he was. The passion he brought to each jersey, particularly the Ireland one, will never be forgotten. He played with an amazing spirit and a never say die attitude.

'As a father he brought those same qualities that he had on the pitch into his personal life. Although a shy and reserved character, my father was a genuine and endearing person to be around. Anyone that had the fortune to meet him would agree.

'He was and still is humble about the great career that he had. While some would shout from the rooftops about playing for their country, my dad went about his business preferring not to brag, even though he could have.

'I haven't met many people who dislike my father. I'm proud of him, for what he had achieved and for sticking through the hard times when many a person would have quit. My father proved he isn't a quitter. He is a genuine good guy and will be forever.'

The words of Dawn

Dave's partner now is Dawn, who met him not when he was an upcoming highly rated full-back at Derby or when he was on his way to Oxford to claim his first medals in English football, but when he was probably at his lowest ebb in life yet somehow they have managed to build an incredible life together.

'It's funny but when I first met Dave he introduced himself to me as Frank. I had no idea who he was especially that he was once a famous footballer. Even now he is Frank to me, my daughter calls him Frank, I actually only call him Dave if I am angry with him although for the sake of this interview I will call him Dave, I don't want to confuse people.

'Once I found out about his past, it started to fascinate and amaze me especially as not only was he such a good footballer who had achieved so much in the game but that he rarely talked about it and didn't even want to be known as Dave, I couldn't understand why he wanted to forget football, it was such a large part of his life. If people recognise him, and I have been there when this has happened, he will turn to them and say he's Frank that Dave is his brother, it amazing to see just how humble he is about it all. Most retired footballers would be shouting from the rafters about what they had achieved in the game, more so if they have achieved what Dave had. But not Dave, he was different and it was one of the things I liked about him when I met him.

'Dave typically doesn't like speaking about his past life however once you can get him started talking about his life as a footballer it really is amazing, he is such a great story teller and you could literally spend hours listening to him.

'He is so interesting; some of the stories are very emotional especially when he talks about failing while at Peterborough. We live here now and it pains me to see how angry he is that he struggled at the club, he says he is embarrassed by the way he played there but he shouldn't be. He is so humble especially when you think of the life he led.

'I remember when I first started seeing him, a colleague of my mine Barry Sheen told me about Dave the footballer, I couldn't believe it and then I looked on the net and I realised that this man I was seeing had played against Maradona, it was unbelievable. I saw photos of him as a player and I couldn't believe it.

'After we were married about two to three weeks, Dave opened up to me and told me everything, it was a hard thing for him to do but it was important.

'One of my favourite things about Dave is his relationship with his family, for me being an English girl, they are your typical Irish family and are all very close. You can ring them any time and they are always on the other end of the phone willing to give their support, they are always there for him and it's great that he can rely on them.

'I think Dave just wants to be allowed to be who he is, he was always trying to please people but that's his way, he wants to please people that's what sets him out and makes him different. Of course he has made mistakes in his life, we all have but I think Dave has learned from them and he is a happier, stronger person this time round.

'Dave is very hard on himself especially his life as a footballer and how he messed up his marriages but you have to remember it's a two way street and quite often the women out there were more interested in the lifestyle than the man.

'It breaks my heart to see Dave struggle with his back and knees, one of my main aims is for us to move to a bungalow so that he doesn't have to struggle with the stairs. Every step he takes really hurts him and you can see it in his face, I think in the next few years his knees are going to get worse and I worry that I won't be in the house and he'll be on the stairs and they could give way.

'We try and go out for walks to loosen up his legs however in the winter it's tough and we walk less which leads to more pain as he stiffens up, it really is hard to bear for Dave. Thankfully these days his back doesn't cause as much trouble as his knees but it's something that we constantly have to live with.

'Dave gave his all for Ireland, even listening to him now you realise how much playing for Ireland meant to him however sadly for him he just missed out on the most important time. Missing the European championships is where he thinks it all went wrong and is the one thing that still riles him to this day.'

Audrey's words:

'I am the go to person for Dave when he wants to get stuff done. I do all the dirty work that needs doing. Ever since we were young and I would have to go get his comics or head out to the front door to tell John Wilkes that he wasn't around when they would call round to talk to him about going over to England.

'The minute Dave heard the bell, he knew it was them and would tell me go out to the door and tell them "I'm up the field playing football". But being honest I never minded and I would do anything for Dave.

'My mother worried herself sick about Dave, especially with the injuries. I remember every Saturday we would head down to John's Lane Church, my mother went to Mass there for 35 years, and she would have Fr Shaughnessy say a prayer for him. She used also to do a weekly petition for Dave at the Novena on a Saturday. I know Dave often wrote to him too.

'My mother used to pray to Saint Rita, who was the Saint of Lost and Impossible causes, to ask that Dave would be okay. Fr Shaughnessy would often tell my mother if Rita doesn't hear your prayers then be sure and give out to her and my mother used to. She just wanted Dave to be okay and not to have to suffer.

'About 21 years ago my mother and I actually went over to Italy to Cascia to see her body in a casket.

'Nowadays the most frustrating thing I have to do is the constant contact I have with the FAI over the payment of the benefit dinner money. It has been a very frustrating period for both me and Dave especially having to ring them so many times. I often find it degrading and it made us look like paupers that we have to chase for money that's Dave's and not the FAI's.

'I remember getting so frustrated one time that I rang John Delaney himself only to get through to his secretary who told me he was away. John Delaney always seems to be in a meeting or out of the country if you ask me. Each time I called within minutes someone would call me to tell me it would be sorted soon. I've gotten fed up of doing it, not for Dave, I don't mind helping him but, dealing with the FAI. It was always different people; never the same person yet each time it was the same promises.

'It used to be very hard to see Dave struggling, he had so much and then to lose it all and end up homeless. There were days when he was very low and fed up, I would tell him, "Why don't you just pack it in and come on home".

'He did come home one time and we went down to the council to see about getting some housing but we were told it would take a long time such was the waiting list. Dave didn't even have a PPS number so it was hard for him to go and register for dole as well.

'I think that week at home was hard for him, he went looking for a lot of his old friends but they weren't about, they had all moved on too and were married or living elsewhere. A few of them had passed away too, the likes of Steven Scanlon, Thomas O'Toole and Peter Murray. These were lads that had grown up with Dave but sadly they had passed away very young.

'But in the end his life is over there. It's great he has Dawn now, he has really settled down with her and it's a relief for us all. We still worry about him but don't have to as much. They actually met during one of the hardest times for Dave, so she never knew him as a footballer, she took his washing for him and did it while he was living in the basement of the Town Hall and their friendship developed from there. It's nice to think something good came out of that dark time.

'Of course Dave life's is not all about football, he loves reading books, likes his music and films. *Shane* is his favourite film and I'm surprised he is not writing a book about that film, he knows it inside out. My mother saw the film on her honeymoon on the Isle of Man and she told Dave about it, he has been obsessed with it since, he must have seen it over 400 times. I actually got a text from him the other day, about 2.30pm, he said to me, "Switch to Channel Four the greatest film ever made is on".

'I remember for his birthday one time we got him a picture of Alan Ladd however his wife at the time Debbie wouldn't let him have it up in the house and he kept it in the garage. He has often told me that he and Dawn want to go Wyoming to where the film was made before he dies. He must know every line in the film although his favourite,and we all know this line, is the line "You're a low down Yankee Liar".

'Dave loves music too; he loves the old folk songs. He was always the one that would bring the music for the bus even when he was a young lad. I remember we used to go down to the Wexford Inn off Dame Street to see the Wolfe Tones and the Furey brothers.'

Chapter Fourteen

The final word; Clare Langan – Dave's mother

'I used to ask him how come the other boys could not ask their mothers for the money and he would say, "sure they don't have it Ma", I think though that Dave wanted to be the one that owned the ball, that his ball was the one that scored the goals.

'Even though we didn't have a lot in those days, I used to give Dave the money to get them; I remember one week I gave him my last shilling so that he could get a ball.

'Dave was very honest though he never robbed or took anything that wasn't his. He was a good boy; I was very lucky in that I had five of them and none of them ever robbed. Dave was close to his sisters and they all got on great, he was close to his brother Billy too but they had a different relationship.

'Billy had special needs and used to do his own thing. He had no interest in football unlike Dave but was crazy about music. He loved to listen to records however he always struggled putting the pin on the record, Dave used to help him put the records on and the two of them used to often listen to music together. Dave was very good to him and they got on well, but they were different people.

'Before he went over to Manchester United for his first trial in England, he worked as a messenger on the bike, he loved it and then one day he just got fed up of it and gave it up. He also worked down in Laul's shop in Ringsend however football is his first love and I'm not sure what he would have done if he hadn't made it in football.

'Every week his sister Audrey would go get his comics; *Victor*, *Tiger*, *Jag* and *Shoot*. He loved them all.

'Right up to before he went to England, Dave would do the shopping for my mother, every week. She would give him £5, which was a lot of money in those days and he would have to get everything with it, and he did. Any change that was left over was handed straight back, I never saw him keep anything extra, he was so trustworthy, I could drop a ha'penny and he would pick it up and say "Ma, you dropped this".

'I won't lie England changed him slightly, hard for him not to, he was still a great boy but at times there was a change in him. He was very young going over there, and I think like a lot of the young footballers he got a small bit of a swelled head. Despite what we saw as the change, Dave was always so proud to tell us "I'm still Irish, I'll always be Irish, I'll never change". He was very proud of his roots and where he had come from. He used to come home for six weeks every year to spend time with me and the rest of his family. I used to love when he came home and it was so hard when it came to him going back, we used to both get very upset. I used to be a nervous wreck until I heard that he had returned safely to England.

'It's funny, he has lived for so long in England but at first he didn't want to go, I remember John Wilkes and Gerry Flynn, two of the nicest men you could ever meet, used to come to the house and Dave wouldn't want to speak to them and he would send Audrey out to the door to tell them that he was out playing football and to send them away.

'Dave would tell us "They want to send me away". They knew he was good though and they wanted him to do well, Gerry Flynn was a lovely man, he would call, even after Dave moved over to England to see how we were doing. Both men were very good to Dave, even to this day and he talks so fondly of them.

'I think when I look back at all the injuries he suffered that Dave put himself in the line of fire a lot, he had a great desire and will to win but he was almost too eager, even as a boy he wanted to win, he wanted to be the one that owned the ball. Jimmy Magee used to say that he was like a "greyhound" and he was right. No matter what Dave ate he wouldn't put on weight.

'I worried about him so much when he was in England. In those days we didn't have a phone, so it was hard to get in touch with Dave initially. We would write and he would write back before we agreed that he would ring every Friday. So each Friday we would head down to the phone booth in Ringsend and he would call.

'We didn't have a lot in those days but we were very happy. I reared them all well I think, it's good to come from a good family and I think Dave did. We tried to do a lot of things as a family, eating the dinner together especially on a Sunday. We used go down and watch Dave when he played for Cherry Orchard.

'Dave loved to hear the opinion of his Dad, after every game he would ask "What do you think Dad?" His father was always honest too, he would tell what he did right and what he did wrong. He is dead now, 13 years the end of October, he died suddenly which was hard for us all; he was a shy man but a very proud man.

'Cherry Orchard were great to him they got him his first trial in England. He went over to Manchester United. Dave was very young though, I think he was only 14 and he had no sooner gotten off the boat than he wanted to come home. I remember telling him, just try your best; it didn't work out for him that time though.

'He was 16 when he went to Derby then and a bit more grown up. He still got very homesick but he loved being at Derby, he loved and idolised the manager, Brian Clough. Clough was very good to him, mind he could see that Dave got homesick and when he could he would send him home for a break.

'Each time Dave came home he would end the visit by saying "I don't think I'll go back" and I used to say the same words to him each time, "you made your bed now you have to lie in it". He wanted to be a footballer so he had to make some sacrifices, even though I worried about him I wanted him to do something he loved and was good at and that was football.

'He loved playing for Ireland, he was so proud, as we all were, everytime he pulled on that green shirt. Even though we lived on the doorstep of Lansdowne road, as it was known then, I never went up to see the games. His father, who was so proud of him, and his sisters used to go all right, they used to get tickets off the FAI but I used to stay at home and listen to the game on the radio and pray that he wouldn't get injured. It was same when he was in England playing on a Saturday, we all used to listen on the BBC they had the games on the radio back then and I would be sitting there with the Rosary, praying and worrying. I worried non-stop about Dave.

'As I said Dave was so committed he would always get injured but the worst was when he hurt his back and he found out that they would have to operate on it. The first thing I said was, "No one should ever operate on your back", these operations sometimes they work and sometimes they don't, it doesn't work for everyone though.

'Dave's injuries took their toll on all of us especially his marriages. I suffer from arthritis myself and I am often in pain so I can imagine what Dave goes through, between his back and his knees he's been very unfortunate.

'Dave wasn't happy unless he was kicking a ball and when he was injured he used to get very upset so it must have been hard for his wives and children at the time. Even though he has a wonderful wife in his life now I was still very upset when the marriages broke up. That sort of thing didn't happen over here and it didn't happen with my generation, it's different over there in England though, they all seem to do what they like nowadays but it wasn't like that in my day, you had to work on things then. It's terribly sad to see marriages fall apart though.

'I am about to become a great grandmother now as Audrey's daughter, who is also called Clare, after me, is about to have her first child and Dave has three children in England, however I don't get to see them anymore. Elliot his eldest son used to send a card and ask how we are but then that stopped. One of my fondest memories is watching Dave button up his coat, he was only a little boy then and they were over for two weeks. They were getting ready to go into town and it was nice to see Dave caring about him, he loved him so much.

'When he was younger all right he used to come over and spend time with us. I never forget any of the three of them though, I always send a card on their birthdays and at Christmas and I give them something in it, whatever I can. But I never see them no, it stopped all of a sudden, there was an argument and then that was the end of it, we never got to see them. You never really know what goes on though.

'Just like the injuries took their toll on Dave, missing out on the European Championship of 1988 almost destroyed him, I remember he called me and he was crying like a child, "He told me to go home, Ma, I didn't deserve this". He was so upset, I cried myself.

'He couldn't understand why he had been left out, he had been training with the team and then he was gone. He kept telling me that he should be over there with them.

I would have loved to have helped him but there was nothing I could do, he was over in England and I was here. Dave is a bit on the soft side and he couldn't forget about it and move on. It stayed with him a long time.

'I remember Dave telling me that Jack told him he didn't understand how he had gotten so many caps, I don't understand what he had against Dave but I'll never forgive him for the way he treated him, he broke his heart.

'But Dave is in a good place now and I am happy about that, Dawn his wife is one of the nicest people I have ever met and I don't have to worry about Dave as much now. I am forever thanking her for minding and looking after him – she always tells me "don't worry I'll look after him for you".

'She is very down to earth and she's a great worker, I think some of his other wives may have wanted to be with footballers, they were very extravagant and wanted the best of everything. Dawn is not a bit shy, which is great for Dave and I hope she won't mind me talking up her singing but she does a lovely version of *Puppet On A String*. She should be on the X-Factor.

'Joking aside though I'm not sure how long I have left on this earth but I am so glad and happy that he has someone to mind him. He has settled down and can't run away anymore.'

The end.

Chapter Fifteen

Dave Langan's career statistics

Youth Clubs:
Bath Rangers
Cherry Orchard

Overall League statistics:
Total appearances: 443 games
League appearances: 394 games
FA Cup appearances: 14 games
League Cup appearances: 30 games
Members Cup appearances: 5 games
Total goals: 7

Appearances: by club:
Derby County appearances:
Debut 12 February 1977 v Leeds United Lost 1–0
Last game 3 May 1980 v Norwich City won 4–2
Total number of appearances: 155 games, 1 goal
League appearances: 143 games, 1 goal
FA Cup appearances: 6 games, 0 goals
League Cup appearances: 6 games, 0 goals

Birmingham City appearances:
Debut 16 August 1980 v Coventry won 3–1
Last game 4 February 1983 v West Ham United won 3–0
Total number of appearances: 102 games, 3 goals
League appearances: 92 games, 3 goals
FA Cup appearances: 4 games, 0 goals
League Cup appearances: 6 games, 0 goals

Oxford United appearances:
Debut 25 August 1984 v Huddersfield Town won 3–0
Last game 4 September 1987 v Luton Town lost 5–2

Total number of appearances: 136 games, 3 goals
League appearances: 114 games, 2 goals
FA Cup appearances: 3 games, 0 goals
League Cup appearances: 15 games, 1 goal
Associate Members' Cup appearances: 4 games, 0 goals

Leicester City (on loan) appearances:
Debut 24 October 1987 v Hull drew 2–2
Last game: 21 November 1987 v Bradford lost 0–2
Total number of appearances: 5 games, 0 goals
League appearances: 5 games, 0 goals
FA Cup: No appearances
League Cup: No appearances

Bournemouth AFC appearances:
Debut 1 December 1987 v Manchester City Lost 2–0
Last game 26 April 1988 v Plymouth Argyle won 2–1 (came on as a substitute)
Total number of appearances: 21 games, 0 goals
League appearances: 20 games, 0 goals
FA Cup: 1 game, 0 goals
League Cup: No appearances

Peterborough United appearances:
Debut 27 August 1988 v Carlisle drew 2–2
Last game 1 May 1989 v Hartlepool Lost 2–1 (came on as a substitute)*
Total appearances: 23 games, 0 goals
League appearances: 19 games, 0 goals
FA Cup: No appearances.
League Cup appearances: 3 games, 0 goals.
Associate Members' Cup: 1 game, 0 goals.
*Dave became the first Peterborough substitute to be subbed against Hartlepool in May 1989.

Honours:
Division Two title with Oxford United 1984–85
Milk Cup with Oxford United 1986

Other clubs Dave represented:
Ramsey
Holbeach
Rothwell
Mirlees Blackstone

Dave's Irish record:
Caps: 26
Games Started: 24
Substitute appearance: 2
Number of Goals: 0
Debut: v Turkey April 1978
Last game: v Luxembourg September 1987
Win per cent: 38 per cent
Draw per cent: 31 per cent
Loss per cent: 31 per cent

Caps:
1–4 Derby County
5 15 Birmingham City
16–26 Oxford United

International manager's caps:
Caps 1 – 2 Johnny Giles
Cap 3 Alan Kelly senior
Caps 4 – 18 Eoin Hand
Caps 19 – 26 Jack Charlton
(Compiled by Trevor Keane)

Date	Tournament	Home/away	Opponent	Venue	Result	Started/Substitute
9 Sep 1987	European Cup Qualifier	H	Luxembourg	Lansdowne Rd	W 2–1	Started
28 May 1987	European Cup Qualifier	A	Luxembourg	Luxembourg	W 2–1	Substitute
23 May 1987	Friendly	H	Brazil	Lansdowne Rd	W 1–0	Substitute
12 Nov 1986	Friendly	A	Poland	Warsaw	L 0–1	Started
15 Oct 1986	European Cup Qualifier	H	Scotland	Lansdowne Rd	D 0–0	Started
10 Sep 1986	European Cup Qualifier	A	Belgium	Brussels	D 2–2	Started
23 Apr 1986	Friendly	H	Uruguay	Lansdowne Rd	D 1–1	Started
26 Mar 1986	Friendly	H	Wales	Lansdowne Rd	L 0–1	Started
2 Jun 1985	World Cup Qualifier	H	Switzerland	Lansdowne Rd	W 3–0	Started
26 May 1985	Friendly	H	Spain	Flower Lodge (Cork)	D 0–0	Started
1 May 1985	World Cup Qualifier	H	Norway	Lansdowne Rd	D 0–0	Started
4 Oct 1981	World Cup Qualifier	H	France	Lansdowne Rd	W 3–2	Started
9 Sep 1981	World Cup Qualifier	A	Holland	Rotterdam	D 2–2	Started
24 May 1981	Friendly	A	Poland	Bydgoszcz	L 0–3	Started
21 May 1981	Friendly	A	West Germany B	Bremen	L 0–3	Started
29 Apr 1981	Friendly	H	Czechoslovakia	Lansdowne Rd	W 3–1	Started
25 Mar 1981	World Cup Qualifier	A	Belgium	Brussels	L 0–1	Started
24 Feb 1981	Friendly	H	Wales	Tolka Park	L 1–3	Started
19 Nov 1980	World Cup Qualifier	H	Cyprus	Lansdowne Rd	W 6–0	Started
28 Oct 1980	World Cup Qualifier	A	France	Paris	L 0–2	Started
15 Oct 1980	World Cup Qualifier	H	Belgium	Lansdowne Rd	D 1–1	Started
10 Sep 1980	World Cup Qualifier	H	Holland	Lansdowne Rd	W 2–1	Started
16 May 1980	Friendly	H	Argentina	Lansdowne Rd	L 0–1	Started
30 Apr 1980	Friendly	H	Switzerland	Lansdowne Rd	W 2–0	Started
21 May 1978	Friendly	A	Norway	Oslo	D 0–0	Started
5 Apr 1978	Friendly	H	Turkey	Lansdowne Rd	W 4–2	Started

A word from the writers

Trevor Keane: I first came across Dave when I was writing my first book, *Gaffers 50 years of Irish football managers* and interviewed him about his time playing for Ireland under Eoin Hand. I had been aware of Dave as a player and knew he was highly regarded within Irish footballing circles so I was delighted to speak with him. I had gotten in touch with Dave through the lads at You Boys in Green and so I was aware of the various campaigns they had mounted to help Dave. I was also aware that he had his struggles.

I remember as we spoke for the first time, I could barely make out what he was saying he spoke so softly. One of the first things that struck me though about Dave was how much of a story he had to tell about himself, his story was so different from that of the normal footballer. Selflessly I put all that to one side as I focused on my own task at hand.

Dave never left my mind though and during the intervening months when my first book came out, my work life continued as normal and I became a father for the first time, I could not help but think Dave's story needed to move from forums and websites to black and white print.

There have been many cases in sport throughout history whereby a Sports person has fallen from the top of the perch right down to the very bottom however I think in Dave's case, he found a bottom that nobody could ever imagine. The fact that even now he remains humble, shy and soft spoken and not bitter and world weary speaks volumes for a player and a man who is unaware of his own success.

Once again Conleth Meehan, who has played a large role in Dave's more recent life, was involved and we spoke about the idea of telling Dave's story. Like any aspiring writer I was full of self doubt and I think if Dave had met me in the days before I approached him to ask his permission to write down his words and tell his story he would have wondered who this mad man was? Thankfully nothing like that happened and we had a lovely chat and he was comfortable enough with me to allow me access to his mind.

My first meeting with Dave, face to face, I flew over to London and he came and collected me from the airport. I was actually very nervous of meeting him and was not sure what to expect, I need not have worried. A friendly face sitting in a black Fiat Punto greeted me outside the airport and I was immediately comfortable in his presence. As someone who is a genuine lover of football and easily star struck when he meets players, past or present, I had to almost pinch myself getting into the car.

Was I really in the presence of a former Irish football international? Had this man played in the top flight of English football? Was I in the presence of a great defender who had won the Milk Cup? The questions were building up, and soon shifted from football to other thoughts – Had this man really been registered disabled? Had this man really ended up homeless? I could not wait to start talking to him, to pick his brain and most importantly to tell his story.

Writing the book was difficult in patches, I am not an award winning sports journalist, I am not even a full-time sports journalist so to take on a massive project such as Dave's was tough especially with a new born baby and a demanding job. My wife Oonagh and little boy Sean in particular deserve credit not only for their patience but also their support through what was a difficult time for the Keane family.

As does Alan Conway, who has a great future ahead of him as a sports journalist and did a lot of work in getting this book completed.

While true fans regard Dave as a hero of Irish football, the wider community were not as aware of him. Dave had missed out on Euro '88 and as such was from a different era of Irish football. Publishers in Ireland, more interested in the bottom line than the telling of a good story; a story that deserved to be told were not interested in the project. It was hard to blame them, the benefit dinner had passed, how would they generate the interest in the book. Dave's brief time in the sun had been and gone.

In the end, it was in the city where Dave made his name, Derby, where a publisher was eventually found, DB Publishing were only too happy to publish the book and with the mother of the Managing Director a fan of Dave's, we seem to have found the perfect publishing house. There were times during this journey when I doubted my ability to be able to do it justice and to finish it. When I read the wonderful foreword by Vincent Hogan, however, I knew our efforts would be worth it and now that I see a finished book I am glad I persevered and I am unsure what I am going to do on a Wednesday without a conversation with Dave.

There have been some great autobiographies of Irish sports people and

Dave's story needs to sit up there with the best of them. I only hope we have done his words proud.

Alan Conway: To me Dave Langan represents everything that is good about sport and indeed life. Courage, commitment, passion, desire and a will to win, Dave Langan has all these qualities in abundance.

Growing up, like many football crazy kids, I first heard about Dave through my father. My Dad would sit me down and regal to me, stories of the dashing, swashbuckling full-back for Ireland known as Dave Langan.

For many years that is how I knew Dave Langan. It is only when writing this book I began to learn more about Dave. His well-documented problems showed him in a different light. That light showed him as a man. A man who took what life threw at him and refused to let it keep him down. Dave should be proud of the man he was, and is, to this day.

Writing a book is never easy. There are so many people to thank. To my parents Mary and Michael and my sister Michelle, thank you for supporting mc from when the dream of being a writer seemed so far in the distance. Your faith and confidence in me helped me to get to where I am.

To my friends, David, Derek, Stephen, Ciaran, Keith, Phillip and Ross thank you for the support and patience you have shown for me while writing this book. I hope you think it was worth it.

My partner Eileen, thank you for being my best friend through this process. Your love and understanding will never be forgotten through this journey.

My part in this book is dedicated to James Lawson. We lost James during the writing of the book and his spirit and memory pushed me when deadlines seemed impossible to reach. This is for you James.

Lastly I would like to thank Trevor Keane and Dave Langan. Trevor has been a huge help, both as a colleague and as a friend. His desire to produce what you are reading was extraordinary. Thank you for everything Trevor.

To Dave, thank you for allowing myself and Trevor to tell your story. You have brought joy to countless fans through your football and this is our little way of giving back. We really appreciate you opening your life to us. I hope we did you proud.